Eighty Exemplary Ethics Statements

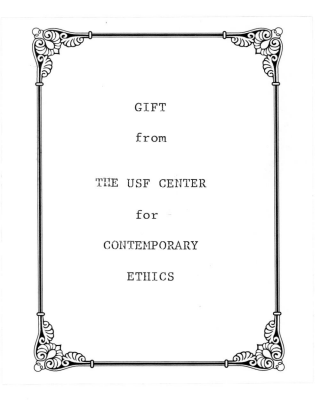

Eighty Exemplary Ethics Statements

With Commentary by Patrick E. Murphy

University of Notre Dame Press
Notre Dame, Indiana
1998

University of Notre Dame Press
Copyright © 1998
University of Notre Dame Press
Notre Dame, IN 46556

Manufactured in the United States of America

Library of Congress Cataloging-in-Publication Data

Murphy, Patrick E., 1948-
    Eighty exemplary ethics statements / compiled by Patrick E.
Murphy.
        p.   cm.
    Includes bibliographical references and index.
    ISBN 0-268-00939-2 (pbk. : alk. paper)
    1. Business ethics. 2. Mission statements.   I. Title
HF5387.M876 1997
  174'.4—dc21   97-28411
                                                    CIP

To the Memory of
John W. Houck
Influential Professor to Thousands
of Future Business Executives
During His Thirty-Nine Years at Notre Dame
and
My Colleague, Friend and Mentor
Who Taught All of Us That Ethical Behavior
Is the Ultimate Bottom Line

Contents

Contents

Contents

Acknowledgments

Several groups of people deserve a heartfelt thank you for assisting in the assembling and writing of this book. First and foremost are the executives from the organizations whose ethics statements are reprinted here. Without their cooperation, this book would not exist. I am indebted to all of them. Several individuals went out of their way to send along additional information documenting what their company is doing with their ethics program.

Second, a number of individuals at the University of Notre Dame were quite helpful in various aspects of formulating the volume. My colleagues in the Department of Marketing have been consistently supportive of my work in the ethics area. A special thanks to Professors Joe Urbany and Oliver Williams, C.S.C., for suggesting specific companies to be included. The staff of the Executive Programs at the University of Notre Dame were supportive in providing financial resources for the copy-editing and development of the book.

Third, our Department of Marketing Secretary, Sandy Palmer, and several students—Ellie Cadavona, Nicole Carlstrom, Jeanne Laughlin, Angela Hendrix and Christy Mommsen—were extremely helpful in entering in the company's ethics statements, proofreading various versions of the manuscript and managing the process of seeking permission to reprint the statements.

Fourth, several colleagues at other universities were of great assistance throughout the project. Lynn Paine at the Harvard Business School was quite encouraging in the early stages and provided several excellent company illustrations. Gene Laczniak of Marquette University offered his usual insightful comments on the introductory and concluding chapters. Bob Kennedy of the

University of St. Thomas also suggested several entries for companies and provided feedback on the textual material.

Fifth, Jim Langford and Jeff Gainey of the University of Notre Dame Press were supportive of my ideas at all stages in development of this manuscript. Their commitment to this work is very much appreciated. Bruce Fingerhut of St. Augustine's Press provided guidance for the book's final layout and was extremely cooperative and timely in making the book become a reality.

Finally, to my family, I offer a special thank you. My three sons, Bob, Brendan and Jamie, are continually supportive of Dad's work and were understanding of the time demands in completing any book. To my wife Kate who has put up with this and many other projects over our twenty years together, I say thank you and really appreciate all you do.

Introduction

Ethical business practice is a noble goal to which virtually all firms aspire. However, many companies fail to achieve this lofty ideal for a number of reasons. Heightened levels of global competition, financial pressures, lack of communication throughout organizations, and the absence of moral leadership at the top levels are but a few of the most prevalent reasons.

The business press regularly reports on the ethical transgressions of corporations around the world. The failings of Union Carbide, Exxon, Bausch and Lomb and others are well known. Rather than dwell on the negative stories, this book accentuates a positive aspect of companies.

The central message here is that establishing a set of formal written principles is an essential step to promoting ethical business conduct in any organization. As the eighty different illustrations in this volume demonstrate, these statements can take many forms. Their exact format is much less important than that they exist and that the firm's employees are encouraged to follow them.

What This Book Is

The volume contains a collection of diverse ethics statements. The word "exemplary" in the title is purposeful. It signifies that these statements are worth holding up as examples for others to follow. As the first chapter indicates, several different types of ethics statements exist. They primarily fall into three categories - corporate credos, values statements and codes of ethics/conduct. However, some are called a creed, principles or vision statement.

An italicized commentary accompanies each ethics statement. The objective is to draw the reader's attention to what this writer believes to be the strongest features of each from an ethical standpoint. The reader is encouraged to look for other significant meanings and messages in them.

What This Book Is Not

In the past ten to fifteen years many companies have written mission statements for the first time. Several recent books (Abrahams 1995, Foster 1993, Jones and Kahaner 1995) have reprinted a number of mission documents. For those interested in studying, developing or revising their mission, these books are excellent sources. While a few of the statements reprinted here have mission in their title, their intent appears broader than just to provide the organization's purpose.

What makes this book different is that it focuses exclusively on the ethical or values statement that firms have written. To this writer's knowledge, no comparable book exists.

This text is not intended to be an endorsement of the included companies as highly ethical firms. While writing and publicizing ethics statements is admirable, it is certainly not enough. A strong commitment to these principles from all parts of the firm is necessary to make the statement come "alive." Several commentaries refer to books and articles that also applaud these companies' ethical stance. The writer has made a conscious effort to include statements of companies who take ethics seriously. However, I have never worked for any of these firms and personally know executives only at a minority of these companies. Therefore, the quality of the written statements is the reason for their inclusion in this volume.

Intended Audiences

Most large U.S. based companies have a written ethics statement (see Exhibit 1 on p. 3). Although the numbers are high in the U.S. partially because of legal incentives and requirements such as the Foreign Corrupt Practices Act and the Federal Sentencing Guidelines, less than 50 percent of non U.S-based multinationals have any formal written ethics statement. However, there are far more small and medium-sized firms or enterprises (called SMEs in Europe) which do not have a formal ethics document. For executives of large companies looking to revise their statements and managers of SMEs wanting to institute one, this book provides ample illustrations of various approaches that can be taken. It is my belief that a strong ethics statement is a necessary, but not sufficient, condition for ethical business practice.

I have used a handful of these statements in lectures on business ethics to students and executive groups (including Notre Dame Alumni Clubs) over the years. The interest is always high in "what companies are doing." As a classroom vehicle, this book could supplement existing ethics texts and demonstrate how companies apply ethical principles in a corporate setting. While the commentaries provide one person's impression, debates and classroom discussion could focus on the relative strengths, weaknesses and omissions of these statements. Use of the text in a classroom setting will also prepare students to make future workplace contributions in ethics code revisions or original formulations.

The serious business reader represents another audience for the book. Hundreds of business-oriented books appear every year and fall into many categories from self-help to inspirational to lighthearted (the Dilbert phenomenon). This book is intended to convey useful information to the interested reader and promote greater attention to corporate ethics by companies worldwide.

Chapter 1
Developing Exemplary Ethics Statements

This book is about ethics statements. Many companies have them, but many are undistinguished or undistinguishable. It takes time to develop unique, memorable and effective ones. This chapter provides guidance for those who want to learn more about their importance, the types and the principles to follow in the process of coming up with an exemplary statement. The approach taken is to pose questions about these areas and then answer them.

Why Have an Ethics Statement?

Many reasons could be offered, but a few will suffice. First, and most important, ethics statements denote the seriousness with which the organization takes its ethical commitments. Words are empty without some documentation. The written statement then serves as a foundation from which ethical behavior can be built. Corporate culture is often viewed as being more important than policies in setting the ethical climate for any organization. However, written ethical principles send a strong signal that ethics matters to the firm. Once an organization's size goes beyond a handful of employees who interact regularly face-to-face, it becomes difficult to convey a sense of an organization's principles and values. An ethics statement makes expectations more concrete. Furthermore, developing such a document forces those engaged in the process, whether they be the founder or current management, to articulate their beliefs in a cohesive fashion and set them down in writing for possible challenge by others. The exercise itself can help to raise ethical consciousness and, let us hope, the resolve to follow the statement's spirit.

What Are the Different Types of Ethics Statements?

Although ethics statements can be classified into several types, three appear to dominate. They are: values statements, corporate credo/creed and a code of ethics. Exhibit 1 shows that the most prevalent is a code of ethics with over 90 percent of large organizations having one, while a values statement is in place at over half of these companies. A corporate credo exists at approximately one-third of large U.S.-based firms. Values statements tend to be relatively recent documents with the majority of the companies introducing them in the past five years and almost 80 percent in the past decade. The credo results are bipolar in that many have been introduced recently while a significant minority have been around for a long time. Codes have the greatest longevity with over 45 percent in place for over ten years.

This section describes each of the types of ethics statements and presents a rationale for them. Recognition is also made of their limitations, and, in the spirit of full disclosure, criticisms are recounted.

Values Statements

Many companies have set out their corporate values in a systematic manner that makes reference to quality, customers and a range of employee issues. Values statements often stem from the company's mission and give direction to it. While these statements are not exclusively devoted to ethics, they do provide insight to how companies integrate ethical issues with their operating principles. Many of values statements reprinted in Chapter 2 speak of a firm's being ethical and fair, with an emphasis on integrity, teamwork, trustworthiness and openness in communication.

Values statements are intended to set out the guiding principles of the firm. Many organizations list them in concert with their mission statement. A number of companies make reference to the values espoused by its founder as ones that have withstood the test of time.

The most frequent criticism of values statements is that companies do not live up to them or that they have no practical impact on the organization. Prospective employees are also encouraged to prioritize their personal values and learn to compromise with the company on some of the less important ones.

Exhibit 1
Corporate Ethics Statements in U.S. Firms

Does your company have a formal written

Corporate credo	34%
Code of ethics	91
Value statement	53

When were these documents first introduced?

	Credo	Code	Values statement
Less than 5 years ago	41%	18.5%	51%
5-10 years ago	23	34.5	27.5
11-20 years ago	14	31.5	13.5
Over 20 years ago	22	15.5	8

When were they most recently revised?

Before '90	19%	18%	17%
'90	25	14	18
'91	25	31	32
'92	31	37	33

How are they communicated?

Only to employees	53%
Both internally and external	47

Does your written code of ethics

	Yes	No
Emphasize mostly information pertinent to your industry rather than general issues	36%	64%
Include sanctions (e.g., reprimand to loss of job) for violating the code	80	20
Contain specific guidance on gift giving and receiving ($ amounts or other detailed information)	84	16

Source: Murphy (1995), 733.

For example, loyalty is a value that some employees follow more than others but it may be compromised with high compensation or severance packages that are offered. It is also important that subordinates understand that the boss's values (which may not be consonant with the firm's) may dictate their success or failure in the organization (Kuczmarski and Kuczmarski 1995) Lancaster (1997) lists the following do's and don't's in meshing personal and organizational values:

- Don't expect too much from your job interviews—talk to persons who have held same job;
- Check outside sources—ask customers or executive recruiters about company; read articles/books;
- Listen to the language—use of words like care and intuition vs. SWAT teams and play to win;
- Ask to sit in on a team meeting—allows person to get a feel for the company and shows interest;
- Don't have unreasonably high expectations—organizations sometimes don't live up to their values;
- Don't be too judgmental—companies, like persons, are not perfect.

Corporate Credo

A corporate credo usually delineates a firm's ethical responsibility to its stakeholders. It is often a little longer than the values statement and is usually written in paragraph form. Among the stakeholders that are listed in most corporate credos are customers, employees, shareholders, communities and the environment.

Corporate credos can serve as a benchmark document for companies which desire a cohesive corporate culture. A spirit of strong communication is essential if the credo's ideals are to be transmitted throughout the firm. Corporate credos are often not precise enough to offer guidance for large multinational companies facing complex ethical issues unless these credos have been extensively communicated over time. Recently merged companies also have difficulty meshing their corporate cultures and coming up with a unified corporate credo.

Codes of Ethics

These ethical statements are more detailed discussions of a firm's ethical policies. Codes commonly address issues like conflict of interest, relationships with competitors and suppliers, privacy matters, gift giving and receiving and political contributions. As noted in Exhibit 1, most large, U.S.-based companies have ethics codes in place and have revised them in recent years. Codes of ethics range in length from a pamphlet sized document of two or three pages to extensive booklets of over fifty pages.

Codes of ethics have long been criticized for several reasons. First, many of the earliest codes were too platitudinous or meant to be exclusively public relations type statements. A second criticism focuses on the general nature of some codes and covers topics that are not especially pertinent to the company or industry. Third, no code could account for every conceivable ethical violation. Another criticism is the code tends to be too legalistic and just codifies rules and regulations rather than provides guidance. A final criticism about codes that they are not enforced. Exhibit 1 shows that 20 percent of the respondents to this survey did not include sanctions for violating the code. Although this number may seem high, it is lower than the 30 percent number that this author found in earlier research (Murphy 1995).

How Should We Do It?

Seven principles that should be followed in writing an effective ethics statement.

Write It.

For several reasons, it is essential that the top management or owners of any organization write down the guiding philosophy or values of the firm. The most important reason is so they can be conveyed to all stakeholders, especially to the employees. If these ideals are not in writing nor articulated regularly, the employees and other stakeholders can only surmise what the principles of the organization are. Another reason is that the statement signals the importance of ethics to everyone who is connected to the firm. Even competitors know where the company stands regarding its ethical views.

Tailor It.

Ideally, these ethics and values statements should be tailored to the organization's industry or line of business. Although most of the short documents contained in this volume are necessarily general, an objective for most companies should be that information pertinent to their firm or industry be included in the ethics statement. For instance, toy companies should make special provision for protecting the safety of children while mail order firms should address their return policies and how they handle damaged merchandize. This writer has addressed the importance of tailoring the company's ethics document in earlier work (Murphy 1989), and it remains an elusive goal for most companies. Exhibit 1 shows that only a little more than one-third of the respondents to the author's survey state that pertinent information is contained in their code.

The code of ethics, which is longer than a credo or values statement, is an ideal place to tailor information. Companies should consider what the most important ethical problems they face on a daily basis and include them in the code. To date, however, most firms continue to provide general information rather than tailor it to issues facing their particular organization. One mechanism that some companies have utilized is to include short scenarios or cases of actual ethical situations that their employees have faced and place them in the code.

Communicate It.

The ethics statement should be communicated to both internal and external stakeholders. Companies regularly distribute these documents to employees at all levels of the organization. Some also make a conscious effort to provide their ethics document to suppliers. Less than half of the companies who have an ethics statement make them widely available to the external stakeholders including customers and members of the general public (see Exhibit 1). The cynical reaction to this statistic is that the company may have something to hide. New employees are usually given the ethics statement to read and possibly sign during their orientation training. However, the ethics statement can be quickly forgotten, if it is never mentioned again. Firms should regularly communicate with all personnel about the code, promote it in departmental memos and meetings on a regular basis. All of the ethics statements contained in this document are communicated broadly, and permission was granted to reprint them here.

Promote It.

It is not enough just to communicate the ethics document. It should be actively promoted. This means that companies should take every opportunity to proclaim its ethics statements both internally and externally. A number of the company documents reprinted in this book are made available in a variety of attractive forms. Some use laminated cards with the values statement and ethics principles reprinted on them. One organization prints its mission and values on the back of the business cards of executives. Still other companies promote theirs in attractive brochures or single pages that can be inserted into a number of company publications.

Many organizations reprint their ethics and values statements in multiple languages, and some are suitable for framing. In fact, several organizations have framed ethics documents hanging in the lobbies or waiting rooms in offices throughout the world. These promotions send strong signals that ethics matters and that all internal and external stakeholders need to be aware of the values and principles that the organization follows. Recently, several companies have publicized their ethics statement in the home page of their website. This is a low cost method of reaching many people and emphasizes the importance of ethics to outsiders "visiting" the company's electronic home.

Revise It.

All ethics statements should be subject to revision every several years. Similar to a mission document, ethics statements should be revised. To remain current, codes, credos and values statements need to reflect changing worldwide conditions, community standards and evolving organizational policies. In other words, they are not cast in stone. In a speech on business ethics several years ago, this writer mentioned that ethics statements are "not the Ten Commandments." One audience member challenged me on this statement and asked "are you arguing for relative ethics?" The response was "certainly not," but minor modifications to ethics statements are sometimes necessary. A number of the statements reprinted in this book have withstood the test of time, but almost all have undergone at least a few revisions. The author was struck by how many of these organizations' statements had been revised in the last two to three years—one as recently as June 1997 right before the book went to press.

Live It.

The litmus test for any type of ethics document is whether members of the organization follow it on a daily basis. One common criticism of all types of ethics statements is that they are not closely followed. If the other guidelines discussed above such as communication, promotion and revision are in evidence, it is more likely that they will be living documents. Top management especially must make a concerted effort to reward employees that follow the principles listed in the ethics statement. What devastates employees is to see individuals "walking close to the line" or openly violating the ethical policy and receiving regular raises or promotions. Rather, companies should willingly take a stand to make the statements come alive.

Enforce/Reinforce It.

To follow up on the last point, enforcement or reinforcement is critical to gain the respect of middle-level managers, their subordinates and all employees of the organization. For longer codes of ethics, sanctions should be specified and timely punishment should be carried out. Some codes simply state that "violators will be terminated," but it is essential that these are not empty words. Sanctions and enforcement for a given violation should depend on their severity. For example, padding an expense account for the first time may result in a salesperson losing commission temporarily, while a manager who induces employees to fix prices should probably be dismissed.

For most of the statements contained in this volume, reinforcement rather than enforcement should be the policy of choice. Since they tend to be shorter values and credo type documents rather than the more compliance-oriented codes, reinforcement appears to be the proper approach because most technically are not enforceable.

Exhibit 2 depicts several concepts that should be followed in developing a code of conduct. These six are quite consistent with the ones listed here. The reason for including them is not to contradict those presented above, but to indicate that organizations should determine the type of ethics statement they desire and select the criteria that best meets its objectives. Since it is an ethics statement, principles such as openness, communicating and living it should be followed closely.

Do Good Statements = Good Ethics?

To repeat: Can good ethics statements be equated with good ethical practice? The technical answer to this question is no, but it is a complicated one. Just following the prescriptions listed in this chapter does not automatically guarantee ethical behavior. Numerous incidents occur each year at companies with ethics

---

Exhibit 2
Basic Concepts of a Code of Conduct....

Uniqueness

For a code of conduct to be effective, it has to be developed by the company to suit its own needs and aspirations. A code must also be consistent with the culture of that company. It is not desirable nor possible to lay down a single model code suitable for all business corporations. A code of conduct is therefore unique and tailor-made for the company concerned.

Open Process

The development and implementation of a code of conduct is an open process carried out in a transparent and high-profile manner. This facilitates staff consultation. It also sends the right signal to those within and outside the company that it abides by a certain standard of behavior in its operations.

Consistency in Standards

Values and principles embodied in the code should be consistent. Double standards undermine management's credibility, cause confusion and erode the effectiveness of the code.

Evolutionary

A code of conduct should address the present day issues, concerns and situations faced by a company. An effective code of conduct evolves over time. It needs to be regularly reviewed to meet with the changes in a company's internal and external environments which may pose new legal and ethical considerations. The way in which the code is reviewed should also be transparent and mentioned explicitly in the code.

Easily Understood

Whatever contents a company decides to include in its code of conduct, they should be written in a manner and style that can be readily understood.

Enforcement

A code of conduct will not serve any useful purpose if it is not effectively enforced. Having the corporate will and determination to do so is the basic requirement. If necessary, supporting mechanisms in terms of drawing up related procedures, delegating responsibilities and creating new organisational set-up have also to be put in place.

Source: Hong Kong Ethics Development Centre, 11.

---

statements. However, a major premise of this book is that statements are beneficial to raising ethical standards. The qualified answer, then, is "hopefully."

Eighty such statements are presented in Chapter 2 from organizations that believe that formal written documents can assist them in striving to make the equation, good ethics = good business, a reality.

Two additional comments are warranted before moving to the statements in Chapter 2. First, the author resisted the temptation to specify what particular principles/values should be contained in effective ethics statements in Chapter 1. The nature of such documents depends on the company's ideals and aspirations, but obviously core ethical concepts should be highlighted. Many models are available in the next chapter. Second, the statements reprinted in Chapter 2 come from firms located in many countries. Therefore, the spelling of certain words (e.g., "organisation" rather than "organization") is kept as it appears in the original version rather than convert it to the familiar U.S. style.

Chapter 2
Eighty Statements with Commentaries

AES

These values are goals and aspirations to guide the efforts of the people of AES as they carry out the business purposes of the company.

Integrity. AES has attempted to act with integrity, or "wholeness." The Company seeks to honor its commitments. The goal has been that the things AES people say and do in all parts of the Company should fit together with truth and consistency.

Fairness. The desire of AES has been to treat fairly its people, its customers, its suppliers, its stockholders, governments, and the communities in which it operates. Defining what is fair is often difficult, but the Company believes it is helpful to routinely question the relative fairness of alternative courses of action. AES has tried to practice its belief that it is not right to "get the most out of" each negotiation or transaction to the detriment of others.

Fun. AES desires that people employed by the Company and those people with whom the Company interacts have fun in their work. AES's goal has been to create and maintain an environment where each person can flourish in the use of his or her gifts and skills and thereby enjoy the time spent at AES.

Social Responsibility. The Company has acted on its belief that AES has a responsibility to be involved in projects that provide social benefits, such as lower costs to customers, a high degree of safety and reliability, increased employment and a cleaner environment.

Commentary

This short values statement stresses four major areas. The first two focus on ethical values which dominate the firm's approach to its stakeholders. The "fun" value is unique but accentuates the fact that work should have enjoyable aspects. Finally, the social responsibility value recognizes that AES does have an obligation to the broader society. If one were to select only a few values to promote, these would appear to be the most essential. The philosophy and application of these values to AES's business decisions are highlighted in a Harvard case on the firm. When the company faced a financial crisis, these values were affirmed (Mavrinac, Paine, et al. 1994).

Autodesk

Philosophy/Values

At Autodesk we work to excite and inspire our CUSTOMERS worldwide with innovative software that defines the market. We strive to produce the best QUALITY products and processes. We're committed to our employees, customers, partners and vendors, as we consider them an integral part of our business. We are flexible in our approaches, practice responsible risk-taking and learn from our mistakes. We're alert to PROFITABLE ideas, and are able to forego short-term gain in favor of long-term vitality for our shareholders.

We are direct, clear and ETHICAL in our communication and actions. We will not deceive anyone—not even our competitors. We speak with HONESTY, courage and care. We're accountable for our words, our work and our processes—building a challenging and rewarding work environment.

We RESPECT individuality both inside and outside the corporation, honoring diverse lifestyles and work styles. We believe our vitality depends on capitalizing on everyone's unique talents. Through collaboration and TEAMWORK we continually create ourselves, our company and our success.

Commentary

The capitalized words in this statement indicate the values the firm holds most strongly. The first paragraph accentuates the business-oriented values of customer orientation, product quality, and profitability. Paragraph two moves to more ethical-related issues. Explicitly mentioning competitors and accountability is rare for these types of statements. The third paragraph focuses on employee-related issues and the uniqueness of individuals is highlighted. The final sentence includes both an uplifting challenge and promise.

Baxter Corporation

Baxter's Values: The Commitments We Share

Respect

Integrity: We build long-term, trusting relationships with our customers, our shareholders, our suppliers and each other, by being honest, open and fair, and by keeping our promises. We live up to the highest professional standards. Our conduct is always ethical and legal.

Respect for Individuals: We treat every individual with dignity and respect, openly sharing information, providing feedback, and listening to each other. Our environment is one of continuous learning in which all employees, regardless of cultural background, gender, level or position can develop their full potential. We value the unique contributions of all individuals, recognizing the diversity of our work force as a competitive advantage.

Responsiveness

Quality: We constantly strive to understand and exceed the requirements of our customers. Our commitment to quality builds customer trust and loyalty, which leads to outstanding results for our shareholders. We provide world class products and services and enhance customer satisfaction every day.

Teamwork: We work openly and supportively in teams, aiming towards common goals. We form teams with our customers and suppliers to respond quickly to changing customer needs. We have fun working with each other and we take pride in our joint accomplishments.

Empowerment: At Baxter, individuals and teams have the responsibility, authority, resources and support to make decisions and take actions. Decisions are made as close to the customer as possible, so that we can act quickly to assure total customer satisfaction. We are accountable for our decisions and actions. Each of us accepts responsibility for meeting the needs of our customers, our shareholders and our fellow employees.

Innovation: Innovation is the key to creating new sources of value for our customers and shareholders. We must quickly transform new technologies and new ideas into products and services that exceed customer expectation We do this by valuing and rewarding creativity, diverse thinking styles and intelligent risk-taking. We act to maximize potential success, rather than to minimize potential failure.

Results

Creating Value: We keep all of our commitments by establishing efficient and effective processes that consistently produce excellent returns for our shareholders and which assure total customer satisfaction. We continuously hold one another accountable for living the shared values.

Reprinted with permission of Baxter International, Inc.

Commentary

Baxter uses the 3 R's (Respect, Responsiveness, and Results) as the theme of its values statement. It seems significant that Integrity is the first value mentioned. The critical role that employees play in setting an ethical climate for the company is noted in the Respect for Individuals value. Responsiveness deals with importance of customers and suppliers in delivering Baxter's products. The Empowerment value places emphasis on the responsibility and accountability of individuals in meeting the needs of stakeholders. Results also focus on generating returns for stockholders and satisfaction for customers. This statement is a very stakeholder-oriented one, and stresses the interrelated nature of ethical and financial goals.

Bayer Corporation

Our Vision

Our Vision is to be a leader in the markets we serve and to be a major contributor to our worldwide parent company. We will achieve our Vision through a diversified, highly motivated work force, by satisfying and retaining loyalties of our external and internal customers; with an organization that fosters teamwork and is unencumbered by bureaucracy; by being environmentally responsible; and by being good corporate citizens in the communities in which we work and live.

Organizational Culture

>Creating an environment that encourages employees to feel a sense of ownership in the business, as well as recognizes dedication and commitment toward our company's business goals

Management Composition

>Developing a highly competent and motivated management group characterized by diversity of gender, race and culture and qualify to advance within the worldwide Bayer Group

Quality & Productivity

>Involving and empowering employees to achieve continuous quality and productivity improvement

Customer Loyalty

>Winning and retaining customers' loyalty by anticipating and satisfying their requirements

Sales & Profitability

>Increasing our profits by maximizing sales of current products and by developing technologies and products to expand existing markets and penetrate new ones

R&D Focus

>Strengthening R&D to capitalize on opportunities specific to the North American market

Expertise with Responsibility
>Applying technical expertise to advance our business, while assuring the safety and protection of our employees, customers, communities and the environment

Capital Investment
>Delivering high returns on new capital investments, turning around weak businesses and divesting consistent non-performers. Requiring each business to be profitable and provide a fair return on investment

Business Development
>Supplementing internal development through acquisitions, licensing and strategic alliances

Resource Allocation
>Achieving maximum benefit and efficiency by sharing resources, information, technology and human resources among all divisions and servicing groups

Values and Beliefs

The realization of our Vision is guided by the following Values and Beliefs:

Our People
>Rewarding performance with fair and competitive compensation

>Investing in employee professional development and personal growth

>Achieving management diversity by gender, race and culture

>Encouraging and recognizing outstanding accomplishments

Our Organization
>Assuring an organization unencumbered by bureaucracy

>Delegating decision-making authority

Fostering teamwork among organizational units worldwide

Our Environment and Communities

Maintaining work environments where employee health and safety are the highest priorities

Developing only products that can be manufactured, used and disposed of in an environmentally responsible way

Taking an active role in the communities in which we work and live

Our Business

Satisfying the requirements of external and internal customers

Maintaining high ethical standards in all business actions

Encouraging and supporting among employees entrepreneurial attitudes, opportunity seeking and applied creativity

Managing for the long term

Commentary

Bayer's vision, values, and beliefs (VVB) combines both sound business principles (i.e., quality and productivity, sales and profitability, and capital investment) and ethical values into this statement. The various stakeholders (i.e., our people, our organization, our environment and communities, and our business) are recognized and briefly discussed. The phrase "expertise with responsibility" in the vision portion has been utilized by the firm in its advertising. Bayer has reinforced this document by putting in place an extensive training program that uses several video cases to illustrate situations where employees can discuss how to apply the corporate VVB to actual ethical problems encountered by the firm.

Binney & Smith

Corporate Values

These are the character and nature of our company that we expect everyone to follow and reinforce with each other regardless of position or level.

Integrity

- Conduct yourself with the highest standards of ethics, personally and corporately.
- Conduct honest, open, and forthright dealings inside and outside the company.
- Conduct fair and equitable treatment of employees, customers, suppliers and the community.
- Conduct yourself and your organization in a fiscally moderate way.

Objectivity

- Make a clear-eyed assessment of facts in a candid way.
- Face up to difficult issues and act in a timely, appropriate manner.
- Speak up freely and openly without fear.

Innovation

- Seek creative solutions to long-range issues and everyday problems.
- Think outside the lines: challenge and encourage others to do so as well.
- Take informed risks on new ways of doing things. Be willing to make mistakes and learn from them.
- Recognize and reward innovative actions and results.

Partnership

- Work with others to achieve mutual, compatible business goals.
- Trust others to say what they mean and to do what they say they will.
- Seek collaboration from others to engender broad-based support for your efforts.
- Provide a secure workplace for our employees.

High Performance

- Produce above-average sales and profit growth over time by consistent execution of our business strategies.
- Outperform competition through creativity and innovation rather than spending.
- Maintain high quality products through consumer sensitivity and stringent quality control procedures.
- Achieve above-average productivity in manufacturing systems and operations, and administrative and organizational effectiveness.

Commentary

The five values singled out by Binney & Smith are notable both for the small number and the elaboration on each. It appears that they follow a natural progression. If an individual possesses integrity, s/he will likely be objective. Once these values are in place, it makes innovation and partnership possible because people are treated in a forthright manner. If the first three values are achieved, high perform-ance in terms of product quality, productivity, sales, and profits should be accomplished.

Boeing

Integrity Statement

Integrity is a fundamental part of Boeing history and of the way we do business. Our commitment to integrity means that all of our actions and relationships are based on these uncompromising values:

Treat each other with respect
■
Deal fairly in all of our relationships
■
Honor our commitments and obligations
■
Communicate honestly
■
Take responsibility for our actions
■
Deliver safe and reliable products of the highest quality
■
Provide equal opportunity to all
■
Comply with all laws and regulations

Boeing Management Attributes

Boeing will evaluate, promote, and retain managers on the basis of the following attributes:

- Has a record of excellent performance with the highest ethical standards
- Is committed to The Boeing Company, its principles, objectives, and goals
- Leads Continuous Quality Improvement focused on Customer satisfaction
- Treats people with fairness, trust, and respect

- Removes barriers, promotes teamwork, and empowers people to improve business performance
- Demonstrates innovation and seeks to improve technical and business competence
- Seeks intellectual growth and learning
- Coaches people to develop their capabilities
- Shares information, listens to others, and maintains objectivity
- Provides timely communication on results and processes

Commentary

Although this integrity statement may appear short, Boeing supports it with many additional documents and the management attributes. Specifically, the company has the most extensive code of ethics this writer has ever seen—in excess of sixty pages. The active nature of the eight values shows that Boeing expects its employees to be proactive. The fact that "Comply with all laws and regulations" appears last signals that these are ethical, not legalistic principles. The firm expects its managers to follow the attributes and beginning with "highest ethical standards" appears significant. Most of the other attributes upon which these individuals are evaluated, promoted and retained also contain reference to ethics concepts. Boeing has been idenified in a recent book (Fritzsche 1997) as a highly ethical company.

Borg-Warner
Security Corporation

Any business is a member of a social system, entitled to the rights and bound by the responsibilities of that membership.

Its freedom to pursue economic goals is constrained by law and channeled by the forces of a free market. But these demands are minimal, requiring only that a business provide wanted goods and services, compete fairly, and cause no obvious harm.

For some companies that is enough. It is not enough for Borg-Warner.

We impose upon ourselves an obligation to reach beyond the minimal. We do so convinced that by making a larger contribution to the society that sustains us, we best assure not only its future vitality, but our own.

This is what we believe . . .

We believe in the dignity of the individual.
However large and complex a business may be, its work is still done by people dealing with people. Each person involved is a unique human being, with pride, needs, values, and innate personal worth. For Borg-Warner to succeed we must operate in a climate of openness and trust, in which each of us freely grants others the same respect, cooperation, and decency we seek for ourselves.

We believe in our responsibility to the common good.
Because Borg-Warner is both an economic and social force, our responsibilities to the public are large. The spur of competition and the sanctions of the law give strong guidance to our behavior, but alone do not inspire our best. For that we must heed the voice of our natural concern for others. Our challenge is to supply goods and services that are of superior value to those who use them; to create jobs that provide meaning for those who do them; to honor and

enhance human life; and to offer our talents and our wealth
to help improve the world we share.

We believe in the endless quest for excellence.
Though we may be better today than we were yesterday,
we are not as good as we must become. Borg-Warner
chooses to be a leader—in serving our customers,
advancing our technologies, and rewarding all who invest
in us their time, money and trust. None of us can settle for
doing less than our best, and we can never stop trying to
surpass what already has been achieved.

We believe in continuous renewal.
A corporation endures and prospers only by moving
forward. The past has given us the present to build on. But
to follow our vision to the future, we must see the
difference between traditions that give us continuity and
strength, and conventions that no longer serve us—and
have the courage to act on that knowledge. Most can adapt
after change has occurred; we must be among the few who
anticipate change, shape it to our purpose, and act as its
agents.

**We believe in the commonwealth of Borg-Warner and its
people.**
Borg-Warner is both a federation of business and a
community of people. Our goal is to preserve the freedom
each of us needs to find personal satisfaction while
building the strength that comes from unity. True unity is
more than a melding of self-interests; it results when values
and ideals also are shared. Some of ours are spelled out in
these statements of belief. Others include faith in our
political, economic, and spiritual heritage; pride in our
work and our company; the knowledge that loyalty must
flow in many directions; and a conviction that power is
strongest when shared. We look to the unifying force of
these beliefs as a source of energy to brighten the future of
our company and all who depend on it.

Commentary

This document originated in the early 1980s when then-Chairman James Bere asked a group of senior managers to help him define the company's basic principles. Based on written reflections and personal interviews, their ideas were grouped into the five belief statements listed above. The preamble was added later. It explicitly notes the obligations of the firm. Terms like "common good" in the second statement and "commonwealth" in the fifth one are uncommon for a business firm. Like many other statements in this volume, the "we believe" points emphasize both economic and social goals. What distinguishes this one is its "we pledge of allegiance" style.

Cadbury Schweppes

The Character of the Company

Cadbury Schweppes earns its living in a competitive world. It needs to do so successfully to meet its obligations to all those with a stake in the enterprise and to make the Company one to which people are proud to belong.

We are in business to meet the needs of consumers internationally for products and services of good value and consistent quality. Our success in doing so is measured by the profitable growth of Cadbury Schweppes and by the advancement of its reputation.

The basis of our business is the good will of our customers, since we depend on literally millions of repeat purchases daily. The Company's main commercial assets are its brands and it is our responsibility to develop the markets for them. Cadbury Schweppes' brands are a guarantee to consumers of quality and value and we must invest consistently in building their reputation.

In setting out what the Company needs to become, I find no conflict between the values and characteristics we have inherited from the past and the actions we have to take to ensure a successful and independent future for Cadbury Schweppes. We cannot however depend on our history to carry us forward. The realities of the market place are tough and demanding and the Company has to be able to respond rapidly to them. We need to build on the Company's undoubted strength and to apply them in ways which are appropriate to overcoming the challenges abroad.

1. Competitive ability

Cadbury Schweppes must be competitive in the market place. To succeed, our products and services must maintain their identity and their edge against the competition. We compete on quality, value and service and so we must make the most of all the assets of the business. This means innovating and taking risks, while using research and analysis to increase the success rate, not to put decisions off. We are competing in the markets of the world, so we need to combine local initiative with dedication to the long-term interests of the Company as a whole. We are competing in today's markets and in tomorrow's, so profit now must be matched with consistent and imaginative investment in the future.

2. Clear objectives

Effective competition demands clarity of purpose. Objectives must be attainable, but require us to stretch our abilities, not work within them. Objectives need to be built from the bottom up, but set from the top down. When unit or individual objectives have been fixed, the debate is over and the focus is on their single-minded achievement. All objectives end with individuals, who are accountable for results and therefore must know precisely for what they are to be held accountable. But since the success of the Company depends on the sum of these individual efforts, what counts is the way they are co-ordinated. Everyone in the Company should understand what their individual and team objectives are and how they fit into the wider purpose of the business.

3. Taking advantage of change

Change is constant—in markets, in ideas, in people and in technology. In an uncertain and changing world we therefore need decisive leadership and trading units which are quick on their feet. We have to look ahead to the opportunities which change presents and to use the past only as a staging post on the way forward. We must accept the risks which attend new ventures; above all we need people with enquiring minds, restlessly searching for new and better ways of advancing the Company. Meeting the challenge of change requires us to adapt to new patterns of work, new jobs and new careers and to seek the training which will make the best of these changes, in our own and the Company's interests. The aim is to encourage openness to new ideas and a readiness to adapt to changing needs.

4. Simple organisation

We must concentrate on the core tasks of the business and justify every support activity and every level of authority on the value which they add to the goods and services we sell. The basic building blocks of the organisation are the business units, managed by integrated teams in direct touch with their markets. All decisions should be taken as near with their point of impact as possible. This freedom of operating action carries with it the responsibility to use the strengths and resources of the Cadbury Schweppes Group where appropriate and to keep the aims of the units in line with those of the Company as a whole. The more straightforward the organisation and the way in which it arrives at decisions, the speedier its response, the more readily it can be adapted, the more satisfying it is to work in and the lower the cost it imposes on those it is there to serve. Building up informal links avoids organisational arthritis.

5. Committed people

The Company is made up of individuals and its success turns on their commitment to its aims. That commitment can only be won through our ability to bring about a convergence of individual, team and company goals. People should know what is expected of them and be given every help to meet those expectations. Our standards should be demanding and demanding standards require appropriate rewards. Belief in the ability of people to grow means planning to promote from within, except when an outside infusion is needed. Equally it means that where we fail with people, the situation must be faced up to openly and promptly and resolved with the least loss of individual self-respect, because the failure is shared. In the same way the responsibility for the development of people is shared, the drive must come from the individual and the training resources from the Company. Everyone in the Company should be encouraged to make the most of their abilities.

6. Openness

The principle of openness should apply in all our dealings inside and outside the Company. It follows that we should keep everyone in the business as well informed as possible within the legal limits of confidentiality. It also implies a readiness to listen. I believe in an open style of management and in involving people in the decisions which affect them, because it is right to do so and because it helps to bring individual and Company aims closer together. The responsibility for decisions rests on those appointed to take them, but if they are arrived at openly, the decisions are likely to be better and the commitment to them greater. Openness and trust are the basis of good working relationships on which the effectiveness of the organisation depends. They imply an acceptance of the mutual balance of rights and duties between individuals and the Company.

7. Responsibility

The Company recognises its obligations to all who have a stake in its success—shareholders, employees, customers, suppliers, governments and society—and seeks to keep its responsibilities to them in balance. We aim to act as good corporate citizens throughout the world and believe that international companies which follow that approach benefit their host countries. We believe in open competition and in doing business wherever there are suitable markets open to our trade. We seek to maintain the Company's reputation for meeting society's legitimate expectations of the business and for contributing to the life of the communities of which we are a part. We support worthwhile causes related to the Company's place in society and we encourage members of the Company to play their part in trade and public affairs.

8. Quality

The key characteristic we aim for in every aspect of the Company's activities is quality. Our products sell on their quality and their reputation is in the hands of each individual and unit throughout the Cadbury Schweppes business. An early Cadbury statement of aims reads:

"Our policy for the future as in the past will be: first, the best possible quality—nothing is too good for the public".

We must always be searching to improve quality and to add measurable value to the goods and services we market. But quality applies to people and to relationships, as well as to our working lives. We should set high standards and expect to be judged by them. The quality we aim for in all our dealings is that of integrity; the word integrity means straight dealing but it also means completeness. Both meanings are relevant in this context, because the quality standard cannot be applied in part; it must be consistently applied to everything which bears the Company's name.

Conclusion

Cadbury Schweppes' concern for the values I have described will not be judged by this statement, but by our actions. The character of the Company is collectively in our hands. We have inherited its reputation and standing and it is for us to advance them. Pride in what we do is important to every one of us in the business and encourages us to give of our best; it is the hallmark of a successful company. Let us earn that pride by the way we put the beliefs set out here into action.

Commentary

This document was signed by Sir Adrian Cadbury, the drafter and Chairman at the time. The first four values pertain to business-related points while the latter four deal explicitly with ethical issues. Committed people, openness, and responsibility are hallmarks that differentiate Cadbury-Schweppes from many competitors. Sir Adrian has written about these points elsewhere (Cadbury 1987). The tie between quality and integrity (#8) is quite interesting and represents an excellent meshing of business and ethical ideals. In an interview with the author, Sir Adrian indicated that he followed this principle when he instructed a country manager who wanted to add a filler to the chocolate in a Third World country to enhance the company's bottom line. Cadbury said, "My name goes on the bar," and we are not going to compromise quality anywhere in the world.

Campaign Advertising Code

The General Principles

I recognize that some standards of practice in campaign communications are essential if we are to maintain rather than degrade a well-functioning democracy in Minnesota. I recognize that campaign advertising should present meaningful information on the candidates and their records, philosophies, positions on issues and leadership capabilities. I recognize that emphasis on personal attacks or sensational "issues" and demeaning photos or video of my opponent increases public cynicism, decreases voter participation and degrades democracy. I recognize that at times it is appropriate to criticize my opponent's record, beliefs, and positions, and that these criticisms must be fully documented and must not be false, misleading or taken out of context. I recognize that any appeal to discriminate based on race, gender or religious belief violates acceptable standards of campaign communication.

I further recognize that some of these general principles will be subject to various interpretations and therefore I commit myself and my campaign staff to the following specific principles.

Specific Principles

1. I take full responsibility for all advertising created and placed by my campaign staff, committees or groups connected with my campaign. I will review and approve all such advertising and will publicly rebuke advertising created and placed in support of my candidacy by independent groups.

2. In television advertising, my voice and likeness will be in the commercial at least 50% of the time.

3. In radio advertising, my voice will be in the commercial at least 50% of the time.

4. In print advertising, including newspapers, direct mail, brochures, posters and fundraising materials, I will display the logo of the Code in a legible fashion.

5. I will not use any photo of my opponent that has been

retouched or modified. I will not use any cartoons, illustrations or drawings that are representative of my opponent. All film or video of my opponent will be run in real time and will not be distorted, retouched, colorized or morphed in any way.

6. I will request, by certified mail, that broadcast stations turn down, any independent expenditures, political action committee or special interest advertising that supports my candidacy. If the stations, in their own interest, reject my request, then I will ask them at least to run advertising that is in keeping with the spirit of the general and specific principles of this code.

You have my word that I will be true to this Campaign Advertising Code.

Signature of candidate _____

Candidate for the office of _____

Commentary

This code was developed by Lee Lynch, CEO of the Carmichael Lynch ad agency in Minneapolis, to curb some of the advertising campaign practices of political candidates. Although it has not received widespread distribution, the general and specific principles contained in the code are ones worth pursuing. The specific principles give precise guidelines that candidates and their agencies should follow. Much of the negative advertising practiced in recent campaigns fail to meet these principles. The requirement that the candidate is expected to sign the code also lends a seriousness to it. Agencies for these candidates probably should be asked to sign it as well.

Canada Department of Defence

Statement of Defence Ethics

As members of the Canadian Forces, liable to the ultimate sacrifice, and as employees of the Department of National Defence having special obligations to Canada, we are dedicated to our duty and committed to:

> Respect the Dignity of All Persons
> Serve Canada Before Self
> Obey and Support Lawful Authority

Guided by these fundamental principles, we act in accordance with the following ethical obligations:

Loyalty

We dedicate ourselves to Canada
We are loyal to our superiors and faithful to our subordinates and colleagues.

Honesty

We honour the trust placed upon us.
We value truth and candour, and act with integrity at all times.

Courage

We face challenges, whether physical or moral, with determination and strength of character.

Diligence

We undertake all tasks with dedication and perseverance.
We recognize our duty to perform with competence and strive for excellence.

Fairness

We are equitable in our dealings with others.
We are just in our decisions and actions.

Responsibility

We accept our responsibilities and consequences of our actions.

Commentary

This statement (developed by a 15-person team) for the Canadian Armed Forces delineates six ethical obligations. It is noteworthy that loyalty heads the list. The others represent significant traits that any organization values. Courage is especially interesting because it notes both physical and moral courage as being important. The statement and corresponding program was one of six featured as exemplary ethics programs (Greenwood 1997). It applies to all ranks and departments— military and bureaucratic. Rosalie Bernier, the ethics program manager, said: "The job is not complete . . . we have to make these values and principles part of everyday thinking."

Canadian Direct Marketing Association

Code of Ethics and Standards of Practice
Protection of Personal Privacy

All direct marketers shall recognize and abide by the seven principles of personal privacy adopted by the Canadian Direct Marketing Association.

Principle #1: Giving Consumers Control Over How Information About Them is Used

1.1 The consumer must be provided with a meaningful opportunity to decline to have their name or other information used for any further marketing purposes by a third party.

1.2 This opportunity must be provided to the consumer before any information is transferred and must be repeated once every three years, at a minimum.

1.3 Third parties are defined as: a) unrelated companies; and b) companies associated with or forming part of the same group where such a relationship is either not obvious or would not generally be known to the consumer.

1.4 In addition to the above, the marketer must remove the consumer's name from all internal marketing lists or lists for rental to a third party at the request of the consumer at any time, i.e. all member companies of CDMA must maintain mail and telephone internal suppression lists.

1.5 CDMA member companies are strongly encouraged to adopt a list rental policy which restricts rental of information to companies which agree to comply with this policy.

Principle #2: Providing Consumers the Right of Access to Information

2.1 The industry endorses the right of the consumer to know the source of his/her name used in any direct marketing program. Marketers must make all reasonable efforts to provide this information to the consumer on request.

2.2 Additionally, consumers have the right to know what information is held in their customer files and the right to question and request correction of any erroneous information. Marketers must make all reasonable efforts to provide this information to the consumer on request. In the case of disputes between consumers and marketers, CDMA will act as mediator and may require that marketers adjust data or annotate customer files.

Principle #3: Enabling Consumers to Reduce the Amount of Mail They Receive

All CDMA members must use the Do Not Mail/Do Not Call Services of the Association when conducting a direct marketing campaign in order to delete the name of any consumer, other than a current customer, who has requested that he or she be removed from mail and telemarketing list. A "current customer" is defined as any consumer who as made a purchase from the direct marketer within the last six months or during a normal buying cycle.

Principle #4: Controlling the Use of Information By Third Parties

The purposes for which information is collected shall be identified by the organization at or before the time the information is collected.

The collection of personal information shall be limited to that which is necessary for the purposes identified by the organization.

All those involved in the transfer, rental, sale or exchange of mailing lists must establish and agree upon the exact nature of the lists' intended usage prior to permission being given to use the list or to transfer the information.

Principle #5: Safely Storing Information About Consumers

All those involved in the transfer, rental, sale or exchange of mailing lists must be responsible for the protection of list data and should take appropriate measures to ensure against unauthorized access, alteration or dissemination of list data. Those who have access to such data should agree in advance to use data only in an authorized manner.

Principle #6: Respecting Confidential and Sensitive Information

All list owners and users must be protective of the consumer's right to privacy and sensitive to the information collected on lists and subsequently considered for use, transfer, rental or sale.

Where a use of personal information that a reasonable person would consider to be sensitive and confidential has not been identified to the individual at the time of collection, then positive consent must be obtained prior to such further use of the personal information (effective March 31, 1997).

The industry recognizes that private personal data, such as medical, financial and credit data must be protected by sectoral regulatory codes.

Principle #7: Enforcement

7.1 The Privacy Code is an integral part of the Association's "Code of Ethics and Standards of Practice" and will therefore be enforced in the same manner as the existing Code. Specifically, any complaints of violation by members—e.g. from consumers or government bodies—will initiate a process of review and hearings by CDMA. Members found to be in violation of the Code will have the opportunity to correct their practices; if further complaints are proven justified, members will be expelled from the Association.

7.2 All CDMA members must designate a staff manager to be responsible for adherence to the Principles of the Privacy Code.

The privacy provisions of the Code were developed in accordance with the privacy principles of the Organization for Economic Co-operation and Development (OECD).

Commentary

This code deals with a specific industry—direct marketing. The Canadian Direct Marketing Association has developed these seven principles for its members to follow. Since privacy and accessibility to their information are issues that are of concern to consumers, this association has addressed them in several of the principles. The Privacy Code is brief but hard hitting in what is expected of the members. Including Enforcement as one of the principles lets everyone know that the CDMA expects members to comply, and if multiple violations are detected, they will be expelled. This association has taken the lead in this important area and should be recognized for its strong stance.

Caterpillar

Caterpillar Code of Worldwide Business Conduct and Operating Principles

BUSINESS ETHICS

The company's most valuable asset is a reputation for integrity. If that becomes tarnished, customers, investors, suppliers, employees, and those who sell our products and services will seek affiliation with other, more attractive companies. We intend to hold to a single high standard of integrity everywhere. We will keep our word. We won't promise more than we can reasonably expect to deliver; nor will we make commitments we don't intend to keep.

In our advertising and other public communications, we will avoid not only untruths, but also exaggeration and overstatement.

Caterpillar employees shall not engage in activities that produce, or reasonably appear to produce, conflict between personal interests of an employee and interests of the company.

We seek long-lasting relationships—based on integrity—with all whose activities touch upon our own.

The ethical performance of the enterprise is the sum of the ethical performance of the men and women who work here. Thus, we are all expected to adhere to high standards of personal integrity. For example, any illegal act ostensibly taken to "protect" the company is wrong. The end doesn't justify the means.

COMPETITIVE CONDUCT

Fair competition is fundamental to the free enterprise system. We support laws prohibiting restraints of trade, unfair practices, or abuse of economic power. And we avoid such practices everywhere—including areas of the world where laws don't prohibit them.

In relationships with competitors, dealers, other local

representatives, suppliers, and customers, Caterpillar employees are directed to avoid arrangements restricting our ability to compete with others—or the ability of any other business organization to compete freely and fairly with us, and with others.

There must be no arrangements or understanding with competitors affecting prices, terms upon which products are sold, or the number and type of products manufactured or sold—or which might be construed as dividing customers or sales territories with a competitor.

In the course of our business, we may sell engines and other items to companies which are also competitors. Related information from such customers will be treated with the same care we would expect Caterpillar data to be accorded, in a similar situation.

PUBLIC RESPONSIBILITY

We believe there are three basic categories of possible social impact by business:

1. First is the straightforward pursuit of daily business affairs. This involves the conventional (but often misunderstood) dynamics of private enterprise: developing desired goods and services, dealing with suppliers, attracting customers and investors, earning a profit, and paying taxes.

2. The second category has to do with conducting business affairs in a *way* that is socially responsible. It isn't enough to successfully offer useful products and services. A business should, for example, employ and promote people fairly, see to their job safety and the safety of its products, conserve energy and other valuable resources, and help protect the quality of the environment.

3. The third category relates to initiatives beyond our operations, such as helping solve community problems. To the extent our resources permit—and if a host country or community wishes—we will participate selectively in such matters. Each corporate facility is an

integral part of the community in which it operates. Like an individual, it benefits from character building, health, welfare, educational, and cultural activities. And like an individual, it also has a citizen's responsibility to support such activities.

All Caterpillar employees are encouraged to take part in public matters of their individual choice. Further, it is recognized that employee participation in political processes—or in organizations that may be termed "controversial"—can be public service of a high order.

Just as Caterpillar supports the notion of *individual* participation, it may, to the extent legally permissible, support committees aimed at encouraging political contributions by individuals. The company itself will not normally make political contributions, even where it is legally permissible and common practice.

Where its experience can be helpful, Caterpillar will offer recommendations to governments concerning legislation and regulation. Further, we'll selectively analyze and take public positions on *issues* which affect the company, when our experience can add to the understanding of such issues.

Overall, it's our intention that Caterpillar's business activities make good social sense—and that Caterpillar's social activities make good business sense.

INTERNATIONAL INFORMATION FLOW

Free flow of information across national borders is vital to Caterpillar. We transmit a large, growing volume of business data between countries: machine and parts orders, financial and inventory information, engineering, and other data. Restrictions on the flow of such information—and on equipment used to send and receive it—could harm the company.

Governments, understandably, want to ensure that their national security and the privacy of individual citizens aren't jeopardized when information is sent abroad. But even well-meant government regulations of data transmissions can become serious obstacles to international business. If deemed absolutely necessary, such regulation should be undertaken carefully and with an opportunity for input by business firms affected.

The Organization for Economic Cooperation and Development (OECD), an international association of industrialized democracies, has developed a set of guidelines that strike a balance between privacy protection and the need to maintain the free international flow of information. Caterpillar supports these OECD guidelines.

REPORTING CODE COMPLIANCE

Before the close of each year, the company's General Counsel will prepare an appropriate listing of senior company managers who are to be asked to report on compliance. Those on the list will be required to complete a memorandum, by year-end: (1) affirming knowledge and understanding of the Code; and (2) reporting events or activities which might cause an impartial observer to conclude that the Code hasn't been followed. These reports should be sent directly to the General Counsel. Reports will be treated in confidence.

Commentary

The above sections of the Caterpillar code reprint but five out of twenty-four sections in the entire document. Since only short ethics statements are reprinted in this text, it was inappropriate to include the entire Code of Conduct here. The Caterpillar code is recognized as being one of the best corporate ethics statements for several reasons. As one company executive who worked internationally remarked to me, "it is our Bible." Furthermore, the document has undergone four major revisions since it was promulgated in 1974. The exact date of each revision is noted in the code. Although sections are contained on important stakeholders (employees, dealers, suppliers, the environment), the ones here deal with competitors and public responsibility which are often not discussed. Furthermore, tough issues like international information flow and compliance are seldom addressed in other codes. The current CEO (Fites 1996) discussed how Cat's ethical beliefs apply to the firm's expansive dealer network.

Caux Round Table

Principles for Business

These principles are rooted in two basic ethical ideals: kyosei and human dignity.

The Japanese concept of kyosei means living and working together for the common good—enabling cooperation and mutual prosperity to coexist with healthy and fair competition. "Human dignity" refers to the sacredness or value of each person as an end, not simply as a means to the fulfillment of other's purposes or even majority prescription.

The General Principles in Section 2 seek to clarify the spirit of kyosei and "human dignity," while the specific Stakeholder Principles in Section 3 are concerned with their practical application.

SECTION1. PREAMBLE

The mobility of employment, capital, products, and technology is making business increasingly global in its transactions and its effects.

Laws and market forces are necessary but insufficient guides for conduct.

Responsibility for the policies and actions of business and respect for the dignity and interests of its stakeholders are fundamental.

Shared values, including a commitment to shared prosperity, are as important for a global community as for communities of smaller scale.

For these reasons, and because business can be a powerful agent of positive social change, we offer the following principles as a foundation for dialogue and action by business leaders in search of business responsibility. In so doing, we affirm the necessity for moral values in business decision making. Without them, stable business relationships and a sustainable world community are impossible.

SECTION 2. GENERAL PRINCIPLES
PRINCIPLE 1. *The Responsibilities of Businesses:*
Beyond Shareholders Toward Stakeholders

The value of a business to society is the wealth and employment it creates and the marketable products and services it provides to consumers at a reasonable price commensurate with quality. To create such value, a business must maintain its own economic health and viability, but survival is not a sufficient goal.

Businesses have a role to play in improving the lives of all their customers, employees, and shareholders by sharing with them the wealth they have created. Suppliers and competitors as well should expect businesses to honor their obligations in a spirit of honesty and fairness. As responsible citizens of the local, national, regional, and global communities in which they operate, businesses share a part in shaping the future of those communities.

PRINCIPLE 2. *The Economic and Social Impact of Business:*
Toward Innovation, Justice, and World Community

Businesses established in foreign countries to develop, produce, or sell should also contribute to the social advancement of those countries by creating productive employment and helping to raise the purchasing power of their citizens. Businesses also should contribute to human rights, education, welfare, and vitalization of the countries in which they operate.

Businesses should contribute to economic and social development not only in the countries in which they operate, but also in the world community at large, through effective and prudent use of resources, free and fair competition, an emphasis upon innovation in technology, production methods, marketing, and communications.

PRINCIPLE 3. *Business Behavior:*
Beyond the Letter of Law Toward a Spirit of Trust

While accepting the legitimacy of trade secrets, businesses should recognize that sincerity, candor, truthfulness, the keeping of promises, and transparency contribute not only to their own credibility and stability but also to the smoothness and efficiency of business transactions, particularly on the international level.

PRINCIPLE 4. *Respect for Rules*
To avoid trade frictions and to promote freer trade, equal conditions for competition, and fair and equitable treatment for all participants, businesses should respect international and domestic rules. In addition, they should recognize that some behavior, although legal, may still have adverse consequences.

PRINCIPLE 5. *Support for Multilateral Trade*
Businesses should support the multilateral trade systems of the GATT/World Trade Organization and similar international agreements. They should cooperate in efforts to promote the progressive and judicious liberalization of trade, and to relax those domestic measures that unreasonably hinder global commerce, while giving due respect to national policy objectives.

PRINCIPLE 6. *Respect for the Environment*
A business should protect and, where possible, improve the environment, promote sustainable development, and prevent the wasteful use of natural resources.

PRINCIPLE 7. *Avoidance of Illicit Operations*
A business should not participate in or condone bribery, money laundering, or other corrupt practices: indeed, it should seek cooperation with others to eliminate them. It should not trade in arms or other materials used for terrorist activities, drug traffic, or other organized crime.

SECTION 3. STAKEHOLDER PRINCIPLES
Customers
We believe in treating all customers with dignity, irrespective of whether they purchase our products and services directly from us or otherwise acquire them in the market. We therefore have a responsibility to:

◻ provide our customers with the highest quality products and services consistent with their requirements;

◻ treat our customers fairly in all aspects of our business transactions, including a high level of service and remedies for their dissatisfaction;

◻ make every effort to ensure that the health and safety of our

customers, as well as the quality of their environment, will
be sustained or enhanced by our products and services;

◻   assure respect for human dignity in products offered,
    marketing, and advertising; and

◻   respect the integrity of the culture of our customers.

Employees

We believe the dignity of every employee and in taking employee
interests seriously. We therefore have a responsibility to:

◻   provide jobs and compensation that improve workers' living
    conditions;

◻   provide working conditions that respect each employee's
    health and dignity;

◻   be honest in communications with employees and open in
    sharing information, limited only by legal and competitive
    restraints;

◻   listen to and , where possible, act on employee suggestions,
    ideas, requests, and complaints;

◻   engage in good faith negotiations when conflict arises;

◻   avoid discriminatory practices and guarantee equal
    treatment and opportunity in areas such as gender, age, race,
    and religion;

◻   promote in the business itself the employment of differently
    abled people in places of work where they can be genuinely
    useful;

◻   protect employees from avoidable injury and illness in the
    workplace;

◻   encourage and assist employees in developing relevant and
    transferable skills and knowledge; and

◻   be sensitive to serious unemployment problems frequently
    associated with business decisions, and work with
    governments, employee groups, other agencies and each
    other in addressing these dislocations.

Owners/Investors

We believe in honoring the trust our investors place in us. We
therefore have a responsibility to:

◻ apply professional and diligent management in order to secure a fair and competitive return on our owners' investment;

◻ disclose relevant information to owners/investors subject only to legal requirements and competitive constraints;

◻ conserve, protect, and increase the owners/investors' assets; and

◻ respect owners/investors' requests , suggestions, complaints, and formal resolutions.

Suppliers

Our relationship with suppliers and subcontractors must be based on mutual respect. We therefore have a responsibility to:

◻ seek fairness and truthfulness in all of our activities, including pricing, licensing, and rights to sell;

◻ ensure that our business activities are free from coercion and unnecessary litigation;

◻ foster long-term stability in the supplier relationship in return for value, quality, competitiveness, and reliability;

◻ share information with suppliers and integrate them into our planning processes;

◻ pay suppliers on time and in accordance with agreed terms of trade;

◻ seek, encourage, and prefer suppliers and subcontractors whose employment practices respect human dignity.

Competitors

We believe that fair economic competition is one of the basic requirements for increasing the wealth of nations and, ultimately, for making possible the just distribution of goods and services. We therefore have a responsibility to:

◻ foster open markets for trade and investment;

◻ promote competitive behavior that is socially and environmentally beneficial and demonstrates mutual respect among competitors;

◻ refrain from either seeking or participating in questionable payments or favors to secure competitive advantages;

◻ respect both tangible and intellectual property rights; and

◻ refuse to acquire commercial information by dishonest or unethical means, such as industrial espionage.

Communities

We believe that as global corporate citizens, we can contribute to such forces of reform and human rights as are at work in the communities in which we operate. We therefore have a responsibility in those communities to:

◻ respect human rights and democratic institutions, and promote them wherever practicable;

◻ recognize government's legitimate obligation to the society at large and support public policies and practices that promote human development through harmonious relations between business and other segments of society;

◻ collaborate with those forces in the community dedicated to raising standards of health, education, workplace safety, and economic well-being;

◻ promote and stimulate sustainable development and play a leading role in preserving and enhancing the physical environment and conserving the earth's resources;

◻ support peace, security, diversity, and social integration;

◻ respect the integrity of local cultures; and

◻ be a good corporate citizen through charitable donations, educational and cultural contributions , and employee participation in community and civic affairs.

Commentary

These principles were drafted as an attempt to develop a true "multinational" code of conduct. Senior corporate executives from Japan, Europe, the United States, and Canada participated in the drafting of it. The Preamble (Section 1) gives the general background, while Section 2 lists the seven guiding principles for firms operating is multiple countries. Section 3 is quite detailed in delineating the responsibilities to the various stakeholders. It is noteworthy that competitors are singled out as a stakeholder.

Centura Banks, INC.

The Centura Commitment:

WE ARE COMMITTED to helping our customers achieve all of their financial goals. Customers are the reason we exist, and we must go above and beyond their expectations to create positive, memorable experiences for them. We must listen to their needs, provide them with creative, appropriate financial solutions and serve them in a friendly, caring way.

WE ARE COMMITTED to doing what's right, without exceptions. Every decision we make, and every action we take, must follow the highest ethical and moral standards. We must respect human dignity, reward outstanding performance and empower our people to make the most beneficial decisions for their customers, the company and themselves.

WE ARE COMMITTED to excellence in everything we do. There is always a better way. We must think creatively, continuously improve and pursue new ideas to achieve uncommon break-throughs. We must thrive on change, shun bureaucracy and strive to surpass our competitors. We must grow our knowledge, learn from our mistakes and emphasize quality in all aspects of our work.

WE ARE COMMITTED to following these principles to make a profit. We must profit to remain in business, grow and meet our responsibilities to all who have a stake in our success—namely our employees, our customers, our communities and our shareholders.

Commentary

This short statement outlines the various "commitments" of Centura Banks. Its customer orientation is the first commitment. The second one emphasizes the ethical standards of the firm. The third defines excellence broadly as including continuous improvement, thriving on change and knowledge growth. Finally, a commitment to profit not only includes the monetary return but also the responsibilities to stakeholders. Concluding with this point is intentional. A commitment to customers, ethics, and excellence should yield profits. This statement is unique in using the theme "we are committed" throughout and signals a level of depth in its relationships that is uncommon.

Ciba Specialty Chemicals Corporation

Vision

Deliver Value

We deliver value for customers, employees and shareholders. Value is created through innovation, productive relationships with customers, and speed and simplicity in everything we do. We achieve this in balance with our responsibilities to society and the environment.

Perform to Win

We appreciate and recognise competence and performance. As empowered individuals and teams in a networked company we focus on results. The perceptions and actions of our stakeholders are crucial for our success. We want to win by being their partner of choice.

Shape the Future

We shape the future of our company and industry. We take the initiative and make things happen, always embracing change as a source for new opportunities.

Our Values

Performance

We demand and appreciate high performance. We set aggressive standards and targets. We recognise and celebrate success.

We are quick to compete for a pre-emptive share of global opportunities. We are not satisfied just to meet goals, exceed last year's actual result or maintain our current market share.

We judge performance by considering financial results, initiated improvements and how well we do in attracting, developing and retaining highly qualified and effective people.

Customer Focus

We are passionate about contributing to the success of our customers. We build mutual success through partnership. We strive for speed, simplicity and operational excellence. We fight costs and delays in all areas.

Innovation
We drive for innovation across organisational boundaries within and beyond our organisation. We encourage comparisons with best in class organisations. We foster target-oriented team work. Change and mistakes are opportunities to learn, improve and increase our competence.

People Potential
We respect, stimulate and develop the potential of our people. We are constantly aware of the face that potential is easily underestimated and under-utilised. We support diversity, as it enriches the potential of our world-wide organisation.

Environmental and Social Responsibility
We act responsibly in environmental and social matters.

Integrity and Open Communication
We build trust through integrity and open communication

Integrity means speaking and acting honestly and truthfully. Integrity honours commitments and promises. It is based on trust and competence and rejects politics.

Commentary

This vision and values statement was developed in 1997 after the merger of Ciba-Geigy with Sandoz. The Swiss-based multinational focuses on its three vision areas with emphasis on striking a balance at the end of the first one. Responsibility, both environmental and social, and Integrity and Open Communication are the final two values mentioned and make a strong statement for including ethical concerns with the more business-related ones.

CMS Energy

Our Creed

We, The People of CMS Energy and Consumer Energy, believe that providing superior service and excellent value to our customers, in a safe way, are our most important priorities.

In doing so, we maximize the likelihood of a prosperous company that can provide substantial benefits to our shareholders, employees, and communities we serve.

In conducting our business, we pledge the following to our customers, employees, shareholders, regulators and other government officials, suppliers, and neighbors:

⇔ TO COMMUNICATE honestly and conduct our business with the highest standards of ethics, trust, and integrity.

⇔ TO RESPECT the dignity of the individual, nurture diversity, facilitate training and career development, and promote employee fulfillment.

⇔ TO PROMOTE a sense of ownership, accountability, and responsibility for the company's success by recognizing and encouraging achievement and excellence.

⇔ TO STRIVE constantly to improve our performance by encouraging innovation, responsible risk-taking, and teamwork among all who contribute to our success.

⇔ TO STRIVE to achieve a superior return to our shareholders to encourage their continued support and investment.

⇔ TO PROVIDE a safe, clean, and productive work environment.

⇔ TO PROTECT the environment, and the locations where we operate to preserve them for the benefit of the communities we serve.

⇔ TO BE GOOD corporate citizens through charitable giving and voluntary service to our communities, our state and our nation.

Commentary

The format of the CMS Creed is different in that the active nature of these activities are stressed by beginning each with "to . . .". This document is meant to be combined with the company's vision, goals and strategies statements. However, those focus exclusively on financial and business issues. These eight elements of the creed touch on relationships with employees, customers, shareholders, the environment and communities. The first two on communication and respect set the tone for the creed in that ethical practices are given priority in the firm.

Coachmen Industries, Inc.

GUIDING PRINCIPLES

Fundamental to success for the Company are those basic values which have guided our progress since our founding.

"Our Corporate motto is "Dedicated to the Enrichment of Your Life."

This means we will do our best to provide quality products and services which will improve the lifestyle of our users.

"Our word is our bond."

Our dealers and suppliers are our partners. We endeavor to practice the Golden Rule in all of our relations with others.

"Quality is our first priority."

We must achieve customer satisfaction by building quality products. This will allow us to compete effectively in the marketplace. We will always remember: No sale is a good sale for Coachmen unless it fulfills our customers' expectations.

"Customers are the focus of everything we do."

As a Company we must never lose sight of the commitment we make to those who buy our products. Our deep-seated philosophy is that "Business goes where it is invited and stays where it is well cared for."

"Integrity is our commitment."

The conduct of our Company's affairs must be pursued in a manner that commands respect for its honesty and integrity.

"Profits are required for the company to grow and flourish."

Profits are our report card of how well we provide customers with the best products for their needs.

Our doors are always open to men and women who can contribute to our fulfillment of these goals.

Commentary

These six principles clearly demarcate the values of Coachmen Industries. Quality, customer focus and profits are all drivers for the

---

company. The ethical underpinnings of these principles are evident too—the Golden Rule is explicitly mentioned, customer satisfaction is built on honestly meeting expectations, doing business is a privilege and integrity a major principle. The final sentence presents both a challenge and opportunity to prospective employees.

Comerica Incorporated

Vision

We define ourselves as a relationship-driven financial services organization. Our customers are our first priority. Our employees will be known for their teamwork and will be faithful to our core values and beliefs. We are leaders in the communities we serve. Our board of directors are the shareholders' representatives; we are accountable to them. We will consistently produce returns on equity in the top quintile of the top U.S. bank holding companies.

Purpose

We are in business to enrich peoples' lives.

Core Values and Beliefs

Comerica is a company where. . . integrity, trust and open communication prevail; customer needs drive our business—we strive to exceed their expectations; we value lasting relationships with our customers, employees, communities and shareholders; we are colleagues, respecting each other and working as a team; we are innovative, flexible and constantly striving to improve; we are entrusted with our responsibilities, held accountable and rewarded fairly; and we are proud to be members of the team and enjoy coming to work.

Commentary

This short document captures the essence of Comerica's ethical beliefs. In the vision portion, the importance of relationships (which are inherently ethical in nature—Murphy, Wood and Laczniak 1996) is noted. The priorities given to stakeholders is clear from the vision. The purpose is brief, but very uplifting. The core values and beliefs also place strong emphasis on ethical principles and aspirations. The use of the word "accountable" in two of the three is unique and sends a signal that the values will be upheld.

The Co-Operative Bank

Following extensive consultation with our customers, with regard to how their money should and should not be invested, the Bank's position is that:

• **It will not invest** in or supply financial services to any regime or organisation which oppresses the human spirit, takes away the rights of individuals or manufactures any instrument of torture.

• **It will not finance** or in any way facilitate the manufacture or sale of weapons to any country which has an oppressive regime.

• **It will actively seek** and support the business of organisations which promote the concept of "Fair Trade" i.e. trade which regards the welfare and interest of local communities around the world.

• **It will encourage** business customers to take a pro-active stance on the environmental impact of their own activities, and will invest in companies and organisations that avoid repeated damage of the environment.

• **It will actively** seek out individuals, commercial enterprises and non-commercial organisations which have a complementary ethical stance.

• **It will welcome** suppliers whose activities are compatible with its Ethical Policy.

• **It will not speculate** against the pound using either its own money or that of its customers. It believes it is inappropriate for a British clearing bank to speculate against the British currency and the British economy using deposits provided by their British customers and at the expense of the British tax payer.

• **It will try to ensure** its financial services are not exploited for the purposes of money

Our Co-operative Ethical Policy

laundering, drug trafficking or tax evasion by the continued application and development of its successful internal monitoring and control procedures.

- **It will not provide** financial services to tobacco product manufacturers.
- **It will not invest** in any business involved in animal experimentation for cosmetic purposes.
- **It will not support** any person or company using exploitative factory farming methods.
- **It will not engage** in business with any farm or other organisation engaged in the production of animal fur.
- **It will not support** any organisation involved in blood sports, which involve the use of animals or birds to catch, fight or kill each other, for example fox hunting and hare coursing.

In addition, there may be occaions when the Bank makes decisions on specific business, involving ethical issues not included in this policy.

We will regularly re-appraise customers' views on these and other issues and develop our ethical stance accordingly.

Commentary

This statement was developed in 1992 (and updated in 1995) by the UK-based bank as part of an overall program on ethical banking. Based on extensive consumer research indicating that over 80 percent felt that banks should have a clear ethical policy, the Cooperative Bank embarked on a repositioning program that highlighted these policies in their products, advertising and company communications. Some of the controversial social issues directly addressed in this policy pertain to human rights, armaments exports, tobacco manufacture, animal experimentation, fur trade, and blood sports. The bank continues with the policy today and has seen significant gain in its market position since introducing it.

Cummins Engine Company, Inc.

Statement of Principles

Cummins is committed to quality, innovation and integrity. This commitment is possible because each member of Cummins follows the highest standards of ethical conduct. These standards are embodied in the Cummins Code of Business Conduct. Individual integrity and strong corporate culture are the best assurances that this Code will be followed.

The Code of Business Conduct is an important foundation for Customer Led Quality. Our pursuit of Customer Led Quality will lead to Cummins being the best there is in products, customer support and business operations, and, as a result, growing our profitability to the benefit of all of our stakeholders.

Our success in realizing Customer Led Quality depends in large part on the trust that our stakeholders—customers, employees, suppliers, shareholders and the countries and communities in which we live and work—have in Cummins.

Our aim is that Cummins will be known as trustworthy in all respects. This means that all Cummins people throughout the world must:

- Obey the law.
- Be honest—present the facts fairly and accurately.
- Be fair—give everyone due regard and respect.
- Be concerned—care about how Cummins' actions affect others and try to make those effects as beneficial as possible.
- Be proactive—take the initiative to address issues before they become problems.
- Be responsible—particularly as a citizen of the communities and societies in which we operate.
- Use good judgment—avoid actions and circumstances that may appear to compromise good business judgment or create a conflict between personal and company interests.

Following these principles on a rare occasion may mean losing some business in the short term. This is a regrettable but acceptable outcome. Over the long haul, this type of behavior will gain us business. People respect and trust this type of behavior, wish more institutions embodied it, and will reward it.

Integrity is the foundation of Cummins' relationships with customers, suppliers, shareholders, competitors, partners, our communities, and each other. It provides us the opportunity to meet the needs of our customers better than our competitors. All members of Cummins—directors, officers and employees, distributors, subsidiaries and affiliates—continually work to develop and protect this critical asset through their everyday activities.

Integrity in everything we do is essential to Cummins' ability to provide an excellent and sustainable long-term return to our shareholders, and to be able to satisfy the needs of all of Cummins' stakeholders.

Our commitment to integrity means that we will exceed the minimum requirements of the law and industry practices. This Code serves as a daily guide to our behavior as employees of Cummins and identifies conduct that is not permitted during employment with Cummins. Violations at any level will not be tolerated, and in some cases could result in dismissal as well as in civil or even criminal liability for the company, individuals, or both.

Some of the areas of conduct are very technical. Many are supported by specific policies in the Cummins Policies and Procedures (CPPS) system, which are available in Documaster or in hard copy at every Cummins entity around the world. Applicable policies, including their Documaster designations, are listed below. If you have any questions about any Cummins policy, do not hesitate to call the person designated in that policy.

Although some areas may be technical or the policies detailed, keep in mind these basic guidelines:

If . . .

- You are uncomfortable with a particular action,
- You would be unwilling to tell persons you love and respect,

- You would not want to see it reported on the front page of your major newspaper,

then DON'T DO IT. Instead, ask your supervisor for guidance under this Code of Conduct, or contact the Vice President—Corporate Responsibility and Public Affairs at (812) 377-3857 or via Mail Code 60901 or the Vice President—General Counsel and Secretary at (812) 377-3520 or via Mail Code 60701.

If you feel pressured, DON'T DO IT and get guidance. You may also make anonymous inquiries by calling the confidential "Ethics Help Line" at the appropriate number for your location.

Commentary

This statement of principles is one section from Cummins' Code of Business Conduct. The bullet points indicate the aspirations the company has for its employees. The firm recognizes that adhering to these principles may cost money in the short run. The central role of integrity is spelled out clearly and the statement concludes with specific advice. The principles are supported by an "Ethics Help Line" which can be accessed from company locations throughout the world. This company has a longstanding reputation for ethical and socially responsible business practices and exemplary leadership in these matters (Murphy and Enderle 1995).

Dayton Hudson Corporation

General Policy

It has always been the commitment of Dayton Hudson Corporation and its Operating Companies (the "Company") to conduct business lawfully and ethically. It is essential that the Company maintain its reputation for ethical conduct in its business relationships. The Company's reputation reflects the performance of each employee.

Each employee of the Company has an obligation to act at all times with honesty and propriety. It is not possible to list all policies, laws, conflicts of interest or prohibited business practices. The best guidelines are individual conscience, common sense and compliance with the law. No supervisor or manager may require or imply that an employee should act illegally. An employee who believes that he or she has been instructed to act in such a manner should inform that person's supervisor, the Operating Company's Compliance Officer, or a responsible executive.

Supervisors have the responsibility to ensure that their employees are aware of the Company's commitment to business ethics and its obligation to comply with laws and the Company's policies and procedures. While it is not possible to develop a detailed set of rules covering all circumstances, this booklet provides a guide to assist supervisors and employees in understanding their responsibilities.

Advertising

We are an honest-dealing business. No deceptions. No shortcuts. No gray areas. Being honest is not only right, it's good business. The trust of our customers is one of our greatest assets. That trust must be reinforced and preserved by our advertising practices. The basis of our advertising is providing clear and accurate information that our customers need to make their buying decisions. Our advertising also communicates the competitive advantages that distinguish our Operating Companies from other retailers.

Advertising practices that must be in compliance with applicable laws include, among others, product information, pricing, comparative pricing, product availability, credit terms, warranty statements, and telephone and mail order procedures.

Bribery

It is illegal to pay or receive a bribe intended to influence business conduct. Our policy follows a higher standard than the law and prohibits any activity that creates the appearance of impropriety or the potential to embarrass the Company. No assets of the Company may be used to bribe or influence any decision by an officer, director, employee or agent of another company or any governmental employee or official. It may be acceptable, with supervisory approval, to entertain or provide minor gifts to a customer or supplier of the Company, as long as they are of nominal value, consistent with good business practices and to not create the appearance of impropriety. However, our general policy is against any such activity.

An employee should never accept money or its equivalent from any customer or supplier. For more guidance regarding the acceptance of gifts, entertainment and related issues, see the "Conflict of Interest" guideline.

Commentary

Only the general policy and two of fourteen sections of the Dayton Hudson Business Conduct Guide are reprinted here. The introductory information makes a good point in telling employees the expectations the company has of them and how they should approach ethical situations. The advertising and bribery areas are rather unique in corporate codes and speak to issues that are very important to a retailing firm which operates several chains of department and discount stores. The advertising section, while only providing general principles, does serve to set parameters for advertising agencies or media which may seek Dayton's business. The bribery section also does not pull any punches and provides guidance for employees in buying and purchasing as well as general management positions. This company is well known for its maximum contribution to charity every year and being a model community supporter. This code signals the company's strong stance on ethical issues consistent with its overall philosophy.

DHL Systems, Inc.

Electronic Media Code

1. BASIC POLICY

As an advanced technology company, we use and exploit electronic forms of communication and information exchange. All employees have access to computers, e-mail, telephones, voicemail and fax machines, and some have access to bulletin boards, wire services, on-line services, Internet and World Wide Web.

The company encourages the use of these media because information technology is our business and because they make communication more efficient and effective. However, the company emphasizes that these media—like all other forms of company property—are primarily for company business and not for personal use.

2. GUIDELINES

The following guidelines apply to all electronic media accessed on company premises, using company computer equipment, or via company-paid access methods.

2.1 Electronic media may not be used for communications of a discriminatory or harassing nature, or for obscene communications, or for "chain letters," or for any other purpose which is illegal or against company policy or the company's interest.

2.2 While occasional use of electronic media for personal, non-business purposes is acceptable, employees may not abuse the privilege for any significant amount of personal business or pleasure.

2.3 Electronic information created and/or communicated by an employee using e-mail, word processing, utility programs, spreadsheets, voicemail, telephones, Internet/BBS access, etc. will generally be treated by the company as private and confidential. However, the company reserves the right to review electronic files and messages and to monitor usage to the extent necessary to ensure that these media are being used in compliance with the law and with company policy.

2.4 Employees must respect the confidentiality of other people's electronic communications and may not read, "hack" into, or monitor electronic files or communications of other employees or third parties except by direction of company management per section 2.3.

2.5 Any messages or information sent by an employee to one or more individuals via an electronic network (e.g., bulletin board, on-line service, or Internet) are statements attributable to DHL Systems. All such communications must fall within the scope of the employee's work for the company and may not disclose any confidential DHL information.

2.6 Any employee found to be abusing the privilege of company-facilitated access to electronic media may be subject to corrective action.

Commentary

This statement outlines the position of DHL Systems (a technology service company to the DHL Worldwide Express organization) on the use of electronic media in the firm. Privacy is a growing concern in many industries (Greengard 1996). This firm is one of the first to provide guidelines to its employees on what is expected of them in using electronic communication. While the code is more directive than most reprinted in this volume, the sensitivity of this information requires explicit direction.

Donnelly Corporation

All companies have goals, plans and standards by which they measure their performance. Donnelly's corporate identity has always been shaped by the values that are listed in this document. As we continue to operate in a rapidly changing environment, it is essential that we clearly express and understand our values. This ensures that we accept personal responsibility for upholding them and that they guide our actions.

We invite you to join us in the exploration of the issues that these values raise and in the work of making them a visible part of everyday life at Donnelly. While this may not be easy work, it is very exciting and rewarding. Let's make it happen!

Dwane Baumgardner
Chairman of the Board

VALUES

We believe these elements to be essential in operating our business.

ONE

We serve our customers with excellence. Our existence depends on them.

TWO

We respect people. They are important and we empower them.

THREE

We are highly productive through participation, teamwork and accountability.

FOUR

We demonstrate integrity, high ethical standards, and respect for the community and environment in all of our actions.

FIVE

We are a manufacturing organization thriving on change, committed to continuous improvement, and achieving zero defects in all areas.

SIX
We have strong leadership at all levels which is critical to our success.

SEVEN
We expand and strengthen synergistic core competencies.

EIGHT
We select products based on strong competitive advantage, high profitability, and global potential.

NINE
We grow profitably to achieve security and above average returns for our employees and shareholders.

TEN
We support long-term cooperative relationships with excellent suppliers.

Commentary

These ten values guide Donnelly and are prefaced by a strongly worded letter from the CEO. They succinctly state the core values of the firm. What does not appear here, but is a significant initiative of the company, is the longstanding use of several "Equity Committees." They insure fairness to employees on questions, such as should workers be required to work on Sunday to fill a customer order. Work teams elect representatives (about 140 company wide) to serve on the equity committees (Singer 1993).

A. G. Edwards & Sons Inc.

Ethics Statement

The highest standard of ethical conduct is expected of all A. G. Edwards personnel. When faced with possible conflicts of interests, we should give preference to the client and the firm over our personal interests. We should not, without management approval, use the firm or our positions in it for personal gain other than our direct compensation.

Operating Philosophies

During 1968 and '69, our top management team spent two days a month for 24 months developing a model for the firm we wanted to be and to which we were determined to commit our careers and our capital. We agreed that building this firm would take precedence over our personal estates or positions.

We committed ourselves to delivering financial services of value to a market we called the "mass, class market" through a network of retail branches acting as agent for the customer. We wanted to be customer-driven, and the agency relationship meant that our first allegiance had to be to the client. We should eliminate any profit centers or incentives that conflicted with the welfare or interest of the client. We realized that this plan would not allow us to manufacture our own financial products.

We recognize that the most important relationship in our business is a bond of trust between the client and the investment broker, and we should build and strengthen this relationship. If we are to be customer-driven, we must listen to our customers and be conscious of their interests in all our decisions.

Our growth should come naturally and involve only people of high character who share our philosophy of putting the customer first. Only after we have found better-than-average quality and a philosophical fit should we then look toward viability.

Profit is not the purpose of our business and should not be sought for its own sake. Rather, it is a necessity if we are to be able to continue to deliver value to our clients, so we must be careful to do what we have chosen to do in a matter that is efficient and cost-effective. We should be more concerned with the client than the competitor.

It is one of our corporate objectives to have fun. To enjoy what we are doing, we must like those with whom we work. In order to do this we must respect each other and work together in mutual trust. To encourage trust, we must strive for completely open communication: management must not keep secrets and must not be defensive when criticized. We must foster an atmosphere that encourages employees to speak candidly and without fear of reprisal. How else can we learn?

It is important for all of us to remember why we are here and to be careful to deliver value to our customers for what we charge them. We should try to do our jobs better each week and to have fun doing them.

Ben Edwards
December 1995

Commentary

The ethics statement is brief but to the point. Customers come first and conflicts of interest will not be tolerated. The operating philosophies document spells out the rationale behind the ethics one. The third and fourth paragraphs note the importance of trust and character in making the firm operate as intended. The objectives paragraph notes the importance of fun, open communication and concludes with an excellent question. Too often, top managers do not articulate the philosophy guiding the firm as Ben Edwards has done here. What is obvious from this philosophy statement is the sense of purpose that makes sense morally and operationally.

Ethyl Corporation

Our Vision and Values

To Be At the Top of Customers' List of Suppliers
In the markets we serve, Ethyl will be at the top of existing and potential customers' lists of companies from which they will choose to do business.

To achieve this vision, we will operate according to the following values:

Respect for People
Achieving our vision depends entirely on the ability of Ethyl's people to contribute individually and collectively, to develop new skills, to work in an environment that fosters pride and to share in the contributions they make toward the success of the company. This success requires a culture that makes it possible for Ethyl people to achieve full potential. Such a culture is based on mutual trust and respect.

Unquestionable Integrity
Personal and corporate integrity are the foundations for all our activities. Integrity is a cherished possession we want never to lose.

Continually Improving Quality
Quality means satisfying customers' needs now and in the future. To do this, we must continually improve the quality of everything we make or do.

Our Partners—Customers and Suppliers
To be at the top of customers' lists, we must become their partners. This means we must share their business goals, champion their interests and link our resources to theirs in anticipation of their future needs. We need and will encourage the partnership of our suppliers in support of our customers' needs and goals as well.

Safety and Environmental Responsibility
It is Ethyl's goal to provide workplaces for employees that are safe, healthy and environmentally sound. Likewise, our presence

in communities will not adversely affect the safety, health or
environment of our neighbors. Finally, we will participate in
ongoing activities, like Responsible Care®, that improve the
health, safety and environment of the world.

Good Citizenship
We intend to be good citizens wherever we have a presence
throughout the world. Good citizens do more than simply
comply with laws; they support causes that help to improve the
community. We will support such causes as a corporation and
encourage Ethyl people to take active roles in answering
community needs .

Economic Viability
To realize this vision, Ethyl must be an economically viable and
profitable organization. As we operate according to our vision
and values, Ethyl will enjoy long-term growth with continually
improving performance.

Commentary

This statement articulates the vision and values of Ethyl Corporation. The vision is clear that the firm aspires to a leadership position.
The use of descriptive adjectives such as "unquestionable," "continually improving," and "good" also signals the company's high aspiration level. Another theme is the central value that stakeholders—employees, customers and suppliers, the environment and
communities—play in the values of Ethyl. The final value of economic
viability is purposely placed last, as the last sentence indicates, because
if the company is true to its vision and values, financial success is a
natural byproduct.

First Bank System

Values

As a company, we value:

Integrity
We are honest, ethical and fair. We tell the truth and expect to hear the truth from others.

Leadership
As a company and as individuals, we take positions and lead by example in all things important to us.

Performance
We know there is no substitute for outstanding performance. We continually seek ways to reward excellence.

Quality
We understand that our customers define quality and we strive to consistently meet their expectations.

Diversity
We value individual differences and work to leverage their inherent creative potential.

Cooperation
We will work together to achieve our common goals. Openness and flexibility are important.

Commentary

These six values and the brief explanation of each clearly articulate what matters at First Bank. The "terse" and "matter of fact" tone signifies what the company will deliver and expects of others. The use of the word "we" throughout indicates a sense of teamwork. Although one might not want to read too much into the order, the fact that integrity is first does seem significant. The other values are also explained with clarity. After reading the document, one gets a sense that this is an organization which has strongly held values.

Fisher & Paykel

Vision

- To be the principal provider of the full range of quality lifestyle appliances for New Zealand families.
- To be a significant provider of quality appliances and related products for Australian families.
- To be a growing provider of quality appliances, healthcare products and other related products to the people of the world.
- To provide services and pursue an investment strategy which realises this vision.

How we accomplish our vision is as important as the vision itself. Fundamental to success for our company are these basic values:

Values

Customers
Our future existence relies on understanding and satisfying our customers' present and future needs. Our goal is to be recognised by our customers as a high quality, innovative and cost efficient supplier, and the best to do business with. We recognise that the next person in the process is our customer.

Our People
We value our family of employees as essential to the success of our company. We aim to develop a long term trusting relationship with each employee, encouraging their contributions and assisting in their personal development and education. In all dealings we will be fair and consistent.

Quality Improvement
We believe in step by step continual improvement of everything that we are engaged in, including our administration, marketing, sales, design, service, distribution and manufacturing. We will

encourage cross-functional communication and co-operation to
aid this.

Suppliers
We view suppliers of goods and services as an extension of our
company, with whom we wish to develop long term trusting
relationships. We expect our suppliers to embrace our quality
improvement philosophy in their dealings with us.

Shareholders
We aim to be a company in whom our shareholders have trust
and pride. We will keep our shareholders properly informed of
our company's performance and prospects. We recognise the
need to provide our shareholders with an excellent return on
investment, consistent with long term growth.

Planning
All short term decisions will be consistent with long term
objectives that balance the needs of our people, customers,
suppliers and shareholders. Each year these objectives will be
widely communicated within our company.

Products and Services
We are viewed at large by our end products and services. We
will endeavor to produce technologically advanced products
and services that offer superior value. Continued innovation and
improvement are critical to our survival and growth.

Environment
Reflecting our commitment to a cleaner world, we aim to
develop products and manufacturing processes which are as
friendly to the environment as practicable.

Society
We will conduct our business at all times in a fair, ethical,
consistent and professional manner. We accept our
responsibilities to be a responsible community neighbour, and
will continue to support community affairs.

Commentary

This New Zealand-based firm articulates its vision and values in this statement. The vision stresses the company's role in the appliance market. Although the values do not explicitly mention ethical concepts in the headings, several do make reference to "long term trusting relationships" in reference to Our People and Suppliers as well as "trust and pride" for Shareholders. The last statement referring to Society represents a very clear commitment to ethics and responsible behavior. Fisher & Paykel appear to take their duty to society very seriously by repeating the word responsible/responsibilities in the final sentence.

Gates Rubber Company

Values

At the Gates Rubber Company we value . . .

⟺ ethical behavior.

⟺ quality and service to our customers, both internal and external.

⟺ open and effective communication.

⟺ innovation.

⟺ contribution of both the individual and the team.

⟺ results.

⟺ continuous improvement in everything we do.

⟺ being the best in all we do, and

⟺ trusting and respecting all stakeholders in working with our customers, suppliers, each other and our communities.

Vision

The vision we have for The Gates Rubber Company as we progress into the 21st century:

⟺ CUSTOMER SATISFACTION:
an innovative technological leader dedicated to customer satisfaction with constantly improving products and services of superior quality and value.

⟺ HUMAN RESOURCES:
a progressive and open place to work which views the individual as the most important asset for success, thereby continually improving the individual's capabilities through training, systems improvements and empowerment, stressing a teamwork environment while also recognizing individual contribution providing consistent personnel policies and populated by highly skilled individuals with a perspective of being the best in all they do.

⟺ VALUES:
a successful, prudent, efficient company with ethical standards, recognized as a quality leader.

⇔ COMPETITIVENESS:

a competitive company striving to be the best in the industry, controlling costs while growing in sales and profits, constantly expanding product offerings, serving customers on a global basis and being the highest value producer.

⇔ PUBLIC IMAGE:

an ethical and environmentally conscious manufacturer responsive to customer employees and community, recognized internally and externally for quality and value, welcome wherever we go and constantly striving to improve.

⇔ FINANCIAL:

a financially-sound institution with the financial strength necessary to support the strategic direction, emphasizing long-term benefits of investments and recognized as the best value company by all stakeholders.

Commentary

These statements of the Gates Rubber Company combine business and ethical principles. It seems significant that the first point mentioned in the Values section is "ethical behavior" and open communication and trusting relationships with stakeholders are notes as well. The Vision includes two strong references to ethics. The Values area mentions that Gates is a "prudent" company which singles out one of the admirable cardinal virtues and is rarely espoused publicly by contemporary businesses. The Public Image section also notes that the company wants to be recognized as "an ethical and environmentally conscious" firm.

General Motors

Revised Vision and Gifts Policy

General Motors is to be the World Leader in Transportation Products and Related Services. We will Earn Our Customers' Enthusiasm Through Continuous Improvement Driven by the Integrity, Teamwork and Innovation of GM people.

GIFTS, ENTERTAINMENT AND OTHER GRATUITIES

From Suppliers:

Both as a matter of sound procurement practice and basic business integrity, we at General Motors must make our purchase decisions solely on the basis of which suppliers offer General Motors the best value for the goods and services we need. We should avoid doing anything that suggests our purchase decisions may be influenced by any irrelevant or improper consideration whether illegal, such as a kickback or bribe, or technically legal, such as personal friendship, favors, gifts or entertainment.

Consequently, it is General Motors policy that no General Motors employee accept any gift, entertainment or other gratuity from any suppler to General Motors or bidder for General Motors business, including supplier units which are part of General Motors. This policy applies to all employees whether or not they are directly involved in purchasing activities.

There may be rare circumstances where to refuse a gift conceivably could be against General Motors legitimate business interests, particularly in those countries where gift giving is simply an expected social courtesy and is not intended to corrupt or influence a particular purchase decision. There inevitably will be gray areas or situations where the applicability of this policy may not be immediately apparent. For example, very inexpensive mementos, such as "logo" pens, cups, caps or other similar items of nominal value, may be accepted subject to any more stringent policy which your business unit may adopt.

To help in interpreting this policy, several illustrations of its application to hypothetical fact situations are attached. In the final analysis, however, the best course is to decline any gift, entertainment or other gratuity from a supplier to General Motors. Any questionable situation should be discussed with your supervisor to determine how best to handle it. If there is reason for you ever to accept a particular gift of any real value, it should be reported to your management and the gift always must be turned over to the Corporation for display, use or other appropriate disposition.

From Others:

Gifts, entertainment or other gratuities may be offered to General Motors employees by non-suppliers including customers, government representatives, civic organizations, charities, and others.

As with suppliers, gifts, entertainment or other gratuities form anyone who may be seeking to influence General Motors decision-making should be politely declined. Examples of these decisions include the allocation of vehicles, extension of credit, location of facilities, or donation of charitable grants. In some other circumstances, gifts of no more than modest value may be appropriate to accept. Examples of these circumstances include recognition awards for community service or other accomplishments, non-monetary gratuities for speaking appearances, and other types of appreciation for past services or accomplishments.

Modest forms of entertainment offered by a non-supplier may be accepted by General Motors employees provided the entertainment is not lavish, is infrequent, and does not create a sense of obligation to the host. Even in these cases, we should try to pay our own way for meals and especially for other forms of entertainment, such as a sporting event, theater event, golf game, or concert. At a recognition or awards dinner, on the other hand, it may not be appropriate to pay for our own meal, and there are likely to be meals served at occasional meetings where it may be awkward or inappropriate to reimburse the host organization.

With the exception of "official" gifts, entertainment or other gratuities extended by a country representative to a General

Motors representative, it is difficult to imagine any circumstance in which it would be appropriate to receive a gift, entertainment or other gratuity from a government or union official.

Ultimately, we must be sensitive to appearances that any gift, entertainment or other gratuity offered to us by a non-supplier may undermine the objectivity and integrity of our business decisions. We must use good judgment, tailored to the specific circumstances, as to whether acceptance of a particular gift, entertainment or other gratuity from a non-suppler is the right thing to do.

To Customers:

To the extent our customers discourage or forbid the receiving of gifts, entertainment or other gratuities by their employees, General Motors employees are expected to know and honor those customers' policies. Some forms of Corporate-sponsored entertainment are clearly sanctioned to promote enthusiasm and teamwork, for example, in our established franchised dealer networks. Similarly, modest entertainment of actual or potential customers may be helpful and appropriate on occasion to compete on a "level playing field" with other potential suppliers to those customers not having a policy prohibiting receipt of supplier-provided entertainment.

Even in these limited situations, no gift, entertainment or other gratuity should be offered unless:

- It is legal.
- It complies with the customers' policies, as well as General Motors policy.
- It is justified by a legitimate and evident business interest pertaining to General Motors.
- It is reasonable in light of prevailing local business custom.
- It is infrequent.

In no event should we be giving gifts that could be considered extravagant or entertaining in a lavish style.

In addition, we need to exercise good judgment in selecting a gift on those few occasions when it may be appropriate to give one. Certain items are not appropriate "gifts." These include cash, services, product or service discounts (other than as part of an approved General Motors program), loans, or cosignature arrangements. Alcoholic beverages are not to be given as gifts in the United States and may be given elsewhere only if other types of gifts would not be considered fitting according to local custom and if the other elements of this policy are met.

In sum, General Motors can compete most successfully on the basis of the relative value offered by our products and services. We rely on superior performance, quality, and price to give customers irresistible value for their money. Giving a gift, providing entertainment or other gratuity should be done sparingly and never to exert improper influence on the potential customer's decision.

To Others:

There are other important relationships which General Motors maintains and which can impact our business. Two obvious examples are our relationships with governmental officials and union representatives.

Gifts, entertainment or other gratuities should never be provided to a government official without first getting approval in the United States from a Corporate Affairs vice president or elsewhere from a senior officer responsible for General Motors operation in the particular country or region involved. Because of the complexity of relevant laws and regulations and the varying ethical norms, any decision to provide a gift, entertainment or other gratuity, including meals, to a government official should be guided by consultation with the Legal Staff as to what is both legal and acceptable.

Similarly, with few exceptions, it is illegal to provide a gift, entertainment or other gratuity to a union official in the United States and some other countries. You must obtain advice from the Personnel or Legal Staffs before providing a gift, entertainment or other gratuity to a union official.

The consequences for violating a law in these situations, even if done inadvertently, can be quite severe for the individual, as well as the Corporation.

Commentary

In his strongly worded letter to all GM employees detailing this policy, Chairman John Smith singled out the words "earn" and "integrity" from the Vision Statement. He indicated that the gifts policy is intended to: (1) signal the high ethical standards of GM and (2) apply globally. This statement by GM is one of the most stringent of any U.S.-based corporation regarding the receiving (From Suppliers and Others sections) and giving (To Customers and Others sections) of gifts. The policy is reinforced by the use of 14 illustrations which provide concrete cases on how the policy should be applied in practice. The Wall Street Journal (Stern and Lublin 1996) stated that the GM statement is "among the toughest in corporate America."

Mission Statement

Golden Rule is a business corporation that chooses to have its behavior be in all respects ethical. In addition, we want value and want to practice:

hard work

and

promptness in meeting our obligations.

It is our intent to provide our customers with the best long-term value in the marketplace.

We recognize that any large organization will make some mistakes and do some things wrong. It is our commitment to correct those as soon as they are discovered.

These principles guide our every behavior. We wish to live by them, not because they are good marketing practice, but because they are the right thing to do.

Principles

OUR PRODUCT

In living out these priciples, we will provide health and life insurance products that meet the needs of the ultimate consumer. They will be simple, easy to understand, and work well for our customers. Our products will not always be the cheapest, but will provide the best long-term value. They will be the product we would want to provide to a loved one and will work as if it were a loved one using them.

OUR CUSTOMER

Although we may never see or meet our customers, we have a moral obligation to treat them in a responsible fashion- to make our products work for them. Our customer is an individual, not a number- a person who:

* Values the simple, understandable, not the latest frills.
* Understands the concept of good long-term value.
* Appreciates the value of good quality service.

OUR STAFF

We are individuals who share Golden Rule's values and expect to live by them- people who care about our customers and are willing to work hard to meet our obligations to them.

OUR GROWTH

Golden Rule will continue to grow by developing mutually beneficial business relationships using traditional and nontraditional methods of distribution which permit the Company to deliver its products to the ultimate consumer. In selecting and developing business relationships and methods of distribution, we will choose alternatives that are:

* Focused on meeting the customer's needs.
* Structured to deliver our products in a very cost-effective manner.

We want these business relationships to benefit the customer, the producer, and Golden Rule and, therefore, expect to compensate the producer reasonably for the marketing tasks performed.

OUR FUTURE

The result is more than mere "success"; it is an accelerating cycle of success- the kind of self-renewing momentum that seems to give rise to an industry leader. As Golden Rule products reach more and more people, the Golden Rule reputation for integrity takes root in more minds, and the Golden Rule name gathers ever greater strength.

Commentary

This is a company that attempts to live up to its name. The mission begins and ends with very strong ethical statements. In the five principles that follow, the company tries to be clear that its products are not the least expensive and that the firm has a "moral obligation" to its customers. The Golden Rule staff is expected to follow the principles and growth is contingent on "mutually beneficial relationships." Finally, Golden Rule expects both the name and "reputation for integrity" to insure its long term viability and strength.

GPU Corporation

GPU System's Values

RESPECT
⇔ Be a good listener; encourage diverse opinions and be willing to accept them
⇔ Recognize the achievements of others
⇔ Don't prejudge another person's qualities or intentions
⇔ Respect confidences
⇔ Recognize each individual's human dignity and value

HONESTY & OPENNESS
⇔ Be forthright and never use information as a source of power
⇔ Strive for clarity, avoid "slippery" words
⇔ Focus on issues, not personalities
⇔ Carry no hidden agendas
⇔ Be willing to admit your own mistakes and be tolerant of others' mistakes.

TEAMWORK
⇔ Acknowledge all co-workers in the GPU System companies as valuable team members
⇔ Practice solidarity by respecting and supporting team decisions
⇔ Encourage initiative and participation
⇔ Demand excellence from yourself and seek it from others
⇔ Be accountable to the team

INTEGRITY & TRUST
⇔ Act and speak ethically
⇔ Show confidence in the character and truthfulness of others
⇔ Keep commitments
⇔ Be accountable for your own actions and expect accountability of others as well
⇔ Accept responsibility for your own mistakes and give credit to others for their accomplishments

COMMITMENT

⇔ Seek opportunities for positive and appropriate change

⇔ Be clear in describing what needs to be changed and why, and how that change can be accomplished

⇔ Challenge and change inappropriate policies

⇔ Recognize that taking and accepting reasonable risks is necessary business conduct

⇔ Lead by example

⇔ Demonstrate a sense of urgency in all that we do

Commentary

The five core values of GPU are admirable. In fact, in combining honesty with openness, and integrity with trust makes the list more impressive since many companies include them separately. Each value is explained via the bullet points. The use of active tense conveys to the reader a sense of personal responsibility. If this writer were asked to recommend what ethical values an ideal company should espouse, it would be difficult to improve on this values statement.

GUARDSMARK

CODE OF ETHICS

PREAMBLE

THE GUARDSMARK NAME HAS ALWAYS BEEN SYNONYMOUS WITH QUALITY AND INTEGRITY. COMMITMENT TO EXCELLENCE AND TO THE HIGHEST STANDARDS OF CONDUCT ARE PART OF THE GUARDSMARK TRADITION. IT IS GUARDSMARK'S POLICY TO DEAL HONORABLY WITH ITS EMPLOYEES, CUSTOMERS, COMPETITORS, VENDORS, AND GOVERNMENT. GUARDSMARK EXPECTS THE SAME COMMITMENT FROM ITS EMPLOYEES.

GUARDSMARK IS A PEOPLE BUSINESS. THE SECURITY OFFICER ON POST, THE INVESTIGATOR, THE HUMAN RESOURCES SPECIALIST, THE UNIT MANAGER, THE MANAGER, THE ADMINISTRATOR, THE MANAGER IN CHARGE, THE MANAGER OF BUSINESS DEVELOPMENT, AND THE CORPORATE EXECUTIVE ARE THE COMPANY. AS PEOPLE PERCEIVE OUR CHARACTER, OUR HONESTY, OUR SENSE OF RESPONSIBILITY, AND OUR RELIABILITY, SO THEY PERCEIVE GUARDSMARK. WE MUST LEAD BY EXAMPLE, DEMONSTRATING OUR VALUES AND PRINCIPLES BY OUR ACTIONS.

EACH OF US IS RESPONSIBLE TO EACH OTHER, TO OUR CUSTOMERS, TO OUR FAMILIES, TO OUR COMMUNITIES, AND TO OUR GOVERNMENT. BUT ABOVE ALL, EACH OF US IS RESPONSIBLE TO OURSELVES. GUARDSMARK HAS DEVELOPED THIS CODE OF ETHICS TO GUIDE US IN MEETING THESE RESPONSIBILITIES. ALL OF US HAVE ADOPTED THIS CODE FOR OUR BUSINESS CONDUCT, AND ADOPT IT AS OUR PERSONAL CODE.

EMPLOYEE RELATIONS

GUARDSMARK ENCOURAGES OPEN AND HONEST COMMUNICATIONS BETWEEN ALL EMPLOYEES AND THEIR SUPERVISORS TO CREATE AND MAINTAIN A WORK ENVIRONMENT CONDUCIVE TO EMPLOYEES' PERSONAL GROWTH, CAREER DEVELOPMENT AND JOB SATISFACTION.

IT IS EVERY EMPLOYEE'S RESPONSIBILITY TO:

• DO WHAT IS IN THE OVERALL BEST LONG TERM INTEREST OF THE COMPANY. SEPARATE SHORT TERM CONVENIENCE OR PROFIT MAXIMIZATION FROM WHAT IS IN THE LONG TERM

BEST INTEREST OF THE COMPANY. QUESTION YOUR OWN ACTIONS TO MAKE SURE THEY ARE TAKEN IN THE BEST INTEREST OF THE COMPANY.

• HIRE AND PROMOTE PERSONS ON THE BASIS OF ABILITY. OUR EMPLOYEES WILL NOT DISCRIMINATE BASED UPON RACE, COLOR, SEX, MARITAL STATUS, AGE, RELIGION, NATIONAL ORIGIN, DISABILITY, VETERAN STATUS, SEXUAL ORIENTATION OR ANY OTHER FACTOR, EXCEPT FOR BONA FIDE OCCUPATIONAL QUALIFICATIONS WHICH MAY BEAR ON THE ABILITY TO PERFORM A JOB THAT REQUIRES EMERGENCY RESPONSE AND THE PROTECTION OF PEOPLE AND PROPERTY. WE WILL MAKE REASONABLE ACCOMMODATION FOR PEOPLE WITH DISABILITIES IF DOING SO WILL ENABLE THEM TO PERFORM THE ESSENTIAL FUNCTIONS OF THE JOB.

• ACT TO PROMOTE DIVERSITY, INCLUSIVENESS AND UNDERSTANDING IN THE WORKPLACE.

• ADHERE TO THE COMPANY'S POLICY ON THE EMPLOYMENT OF RELATIVES.

• ENCOURAGE EMPLOYEE DEVELOPMENT. OPPORTUNITY IS A SURE WAY TO RETAIN GOOD EMPLOYEES. COMMUNICATE WITH PERSONNEL ON YOUR TEAM TO HELP THEM ACHIEVE THEIR GOALS AND INCREASE THEIR SELF-ESTEEM THROUGH JOB ENRICHMENT.

• REVIEW NOT JUST THE RESULTS OF SUBORDINATES' WORK, BUT HOW THOSE RESULTS WERE OBTAINED.

• EVALUATE EMPLOYEES ON A FAIR AND CONSISTENT BASIS. ALL EMPLOYEES SHOULD KNOW WHAT IS EXPECTED OF THEM AND HOW THEY ARE PROGRESSING TOWARD FULFILLING THOSE EXPECTATIONS.

• ESTABLISH AN ATMOSPHERE OF TRUST AND CREDIBILITY; PARTICIPATION, DELEGATION AND COMMUNICATION ADVANCE THIS PURPOSE.

• SHOW RESPECT AND EMPATHY FOR ALL EMPLOYEES. EACH EMPLOYEE IS A PERSON WITH FEELINGS AND NEEDS. BE CONSIDERATE WHILE BEING MINDFUL OF YOUR SUPERVISORY RESPONSIBILITIES.

• LISTEN TO THE SUGGESTIONS OF SUBORDINATES AND ACKNOWLEDGE THEIR VALUE.

• MAINTAIN A SAFE WORK ENVIRONMENT.

• MAINTAIN A DRUG-FREE WORKPLACE.

COMMITMENT TO EXCELLENCE

OUR COMMITMENT TO EXCELLENCE IS AS STRONG IN OUR RELATIONSHIPS AMONG OURSELVES AS IT IS IN OUR RELATIONSHIPS WITH OUR CUSTOMERS.

EACH GUARDSMARK EMPLOYEE, AT EVERY LEVEL, HAS A RESPONSIBILITY TO:

• MAINTAIN UNDIVIDED LOYALTY TO THE COMPANY. ALWAYS ACT IN THE BEST INTEREST OF THE COMPANY, AND AVOID EVEN THE APPEARANCE OF ANY CONFLICT OF INTEREST.

• REALIZE THAT THE EASIEST ACTION IS NOT OFTEN IN THE BEST INTEREST OF THE COMPANY. EXAMINE ALTERNATIVES WITH THIS PRINCIPLE IN MIND.

• MAINTAIN COMPLETE OBJECTIVITY IN ALL DECISIONS AFFECTING THE COMPANY AND ITS CUSTOMERS.

• USE COMPANY ASSETS, PROPERTY, AND INFORMATION ONLY FOR COMPANY BUSINESS AND COMPANY GAIN.

• REALIZE THAT THE GOALS OF THE EMPLOYEE, THE COMPANY AND THE CUSTOMER SHOULD BE THE SAME. WHEN WE CONSERVE COMPANY AND CUSTOMER RESOURCES, WE SAVE REAL MONEY. STRIVE FOR CONTINUOUS IMPROVEMENT AND INCREASED EFFICIENCY WHEN USING BOTH COMPANY AND CUSTOMER RESOURCES. SEEK TO REDUCE WASTE AND MAXIMIZE EFFICIENCY.

• REPRESENT THE COMPANY WITH DIGNITY, PRIDE, HONOR, AND RESPECT.

• WORK TOGETHER WITH FELLOW EMPLOYEES TO ACHIEVE THE COMMON GOAL OF QUALITY SERVICE WITH THE HIGHEST STANDARDS OF PERFORMANCE.

• LEARN FROM OTHERS AND SHARE WHAT YOU LEARN WITH OTHERS. RECOGNIZE THAT EVERYONE HAS A CONTRIBUTION TO MAKE.

• RECOGNIZE THAT OUR INDIVIDUAL ACTIONS HAVE CONSEQUENCES FOR OTHERS AND FOR EACH OTHER. EXERCISE COMMON SENSE AND WORK AS A TEAM.

• BE CONSCIENTIOUS, COURTEOUS AND RESPONSIBLE IN BOTH CUSTOMER AND COMPANY RELATIONSHIPS.

• BE SINCERE AND HONEST IN ALL MATTERS.

• HAVE THE COURAGE TO FACE SITUATIONS SQUARELY AND OFFER A DIFFERENT OPINION WHEN NECESSARY.

• RESPECT AND MAINTAIN THE CONFIDENTIALITY OF ALL PROPRIETARY AND PERSONAL INFORMATION OF GUARDSMARK AND ITS CUSTOMERS.

• GIVE ACCURATE AND COMPLETE REPORTS, WHETHER ORAL OR WRITTEN, TO CUSTOMERS AND COMPANY PERSONNEL.

• KEEP ACCURATE AND COMPLETE EXPENSE AND OTHER BUSINESS RECORDS, MAKE CERTAIN THAT COMPANY EXPENDITURES ARE FOR PROPER BUSINESS PURPOSES ONLY, AND ABIDE BY ALL CORPORATE POLICIES AND PROCEDURES RELATIVE TO BUSINESS AND FINANCIAL RECORD-KEEPING.

• RESPECT THE RIGHTS OF CO-WORKERS. SEXUAL HARASSMENT AND OFFENSIVE SEXUAL REMARKS OR CONDUCT ARE UNACCEPTABLE, AS EXPLAINED IN DETAIL IN THE COMPANY'S SEXUAL HARASSMENT POLICY AND IN THE COMPANY'S ETHNIC, SEXUAL, RACIAL AND RELIGIOUS SLUR POLICY. REFRAIN FROM ALL PREJUDICIAL COMMENTS OR ACTIONS.

• ABIDE BY AND COOPERATE FULLY WITH THE IMPLEMENTATION OF THE COMPANY'S EQUAL OPPORTUNITY POLICY STATEMENT. UNDERSTAND AND ABIDE BY THE COMPANY'S CONTAGIOUS DISEASES AND LIFE-THREATENING ILLNESSES POLICY.

• DIRECT ANY REQUESTS FOR CLARIFICATION OF THESE PRINCIPLES OR THEIR APPLICATION TO THE CORPORATE ETHICS COMMITTEE.

• ADVISE FELLOW EMPLOYEES WHEN IT APPEARS THEIR ACTIONS MAY BE IN VIOLATION OF THIS CODE, AND IF APPROPRIATE, REPORT THE SITUATION TO MANAGEMENT OR TO THE CORPORATE ETHICS COMMITTEE. TO THE EXTENT IT IS LEGALLY AND PRACTICALLY POSSIBLE, THE COMPANY WILL KEEP CONFIDENTIAL THE IDENTITY OF ANYONE REPORTING A POSSIBLE VIOLATION.

• CONTINUOUSLY SEEK TO GROW AND IMPROVE FOR ONE'S OWN BENEFIT AND FOR THE BENEFIT OF FAMILY, CO-WORKERS, COMPANY AND COMMUNITY.

OUR CUSTOMERS ARE ENTITLED TO THE HIGHEST LEVEL OF SERVICE AND PROFESSIONALISM IN THE INDUSTRY. THE CUSTOMER TRUSTS GUARDSMARK'S REPUTATION FOR EXCELLENCE; IT IS OUR RESPONSIBILITY NOT TO VIOLATE THIS TRUST.

• DO NOT UNDERPRICE OUR SERVICES JUST TO GET AN

ACCOUNT, AND DO NOT OVERCHARGE THE CUSTOMER. PRICE
OUR SERVICES CONSISTENTLY AND FAIRLY.

• SUBMIT REALISTIC PROPOSALS ON PERFORMANCE, COST,
AND SCHEDULE TO MEET THE REQUIREMENTS OF CUSTOMERS
AND POTENTIAL CUSTOMERS.

• DO NOT PROMISE WHAT YOU CANNOT DELIVER, BUT DO
DELIVER ALL THAT YOU PROMISE.

• BE FORTHRIGHT, FACTUAL, TIMELY AND ACCURATE IN ALL
TRANSACTIONS.

• FACE DIFFICULTIES AS THEY ARISE AND RESOLVE THEM
BEFORE THE CUSTOMER BRINGS THEM TO YOUR ATTENTION.
YOU ARE A PROFESSIONAL, AND YOU MUST REVIEW YOUR
SERVICE TO THE CUSTOMER ON A REGULAR BASIS TO ENSURE
THAT IT MEETS COMPANY STANDARDS, REGARDLESS OF
WHETHER THE CUSTOMER ASKS YOU TO DO SO.

• REPORT CUSTOMER COMPLAINTS TO APPROPRIATE PERSONS
AND RESPOND PROMPTLY TO CORRECT OR RESOLVE
COMPLAINTS.

• SERVICE YOUR ACCOUNTS RESPONSIBLY, HONESTLY, AND IN
THE MOST PROFESSIONAL MANNER. THE CUSTOMER IS
ENTITLED TO OUR BEST EFFORT AT ALL TIMES.

• RESPECT THE CUSTOMER'S CONFIDENCES AND PROTECT THE
CUSTOMER'S ASSETS, INCLUDING ALL CONFIDENTIAL
INFORMATION.

• NEVER USE COMPANY OR CUSTOMER COMPUTING
EQUIPMENT OR COMPUTER SOFTWARE FOR PERSONAL USE OR
TO ACCESS UNAUTHORIZED INFORMATION, AND NEVER USE
ANY COMPANY OR CUSTOMER INFORMATION FOR AN
UNAUTHORIZED PURPOSE.

• OBTAIN WRITTEN PERMISSION FROM THE CUSTOMER BEFORE
USING THE BUSINESS RELATIONSHIP TO OUR ADVANTAGE IN
ANY WAY, SUCH AS REVEALING OUR CUSTOMERS' NAMES OR
IDENTIFYING THE FACILITIES THAT WE SERVICE.

• NEVER ACCEPT ANY GRATUITIES FOR DOING YOUR JOB .

• NEVER OFFER OR GIVE GRATUITIES TO GET OR RETAIN AN
ACCOUNT. THIS PROHIBITION DOES NOT INCLUDE GIVING
CALENDARS, DIARIES, OR OTHER PROMOTIONAL ARTICLES OF
NOMINAL VALUE.

• BE COURAGEOUS AND SUGGEST WAYS A CUSTOMER CAN

INNOVATE AND IMPROVE HIS OR HER PRODUCT OR SERVICE.

EMPLOYEE WELLNESS

GUARDSMARK ACTIVELY ENCOURAGES EVERY EMPLOYEE TO ENJOY GOOD HEALTH AND IS COMMITTED TO PROVIDING A SAFE, HEALTHY, SMOKE-FREE, AND DRUG-FREE WORK ENVIRONMENT. OUR HEALTH IS OUR MOST PRECIOUS RESOURCE. EACH EMPLOYEE, IN TURN, SHOULD:

• PERFORM THE JOB IN THE SAFEST MANNER, AND NEVER PERFORM UNSAFE WORK.

• OBSERVE ALL SAFETY RULES AND REGULATIONS, AND REPORT ANY UNSAFE CONDITIONS.

• REMAIN DRUG FREE AND ENCOURAGE OTHERS TO DO SO.

• ABIDE BY THE COMPANY'S DRUG AND ALCOHOL POLICY.

• IMPROVE PHYSICAL AND MENTAL WELL-BEING.

• BE AN ACTIVE PARTICIPANT IN GUARDSMARK'S WELLNESS PROGRAM, EXERCISE REGULARLY, PRACTICE SOUND NUTRITION AND ENCOURAGE OTHERS TO MAINTAIN A HEALTHY LIFESTYLE.

• SET ACHIEVABLE GOALS FOR YOUR PERSONAL WELLNESS, AND COMMIT TO ATTAIN THEM.

• RECOGNIZE THAT ALERTNESS AND GOOD JUDGMENT DEPEND ON MAINTAINING GOOD HEALTH AND GETTING SUFFICIENT REST.

• SEEK TO MAINTAIN A BALANCE BETWEEN PROFESSIONAL AND PERSONAL LIFE AND TO HAVE FULFILLING ACHIEVEMENTS AND RELATIONSHIPS.

VENDOR RELATIONS

GUARDSMARK IS COMMITTED TO TREAT ALL VENDORS FAIRLY AND WITHOUT PREJUDICE. WE RECOGNIZE THE RIGHT OF OUR VENDORS TO RECEIVE FAIR MARKET VALUE FOR THEIR GOODS AND SERVICES. ALL PERSONNEL WITH PURCHASING RESPONSIBILITIES MUST:

• AFFORD ANY LEGITIMATE VENDOR THE OPPORTUNITY TO OFFER OR QUALIFY ITS PRODUCTS OR SERVICES FOR SALE TO THE COMPANY ON A COMPETITIVE BASIS.

• CONDUCT ALL COMPETITIVE BIDDING IN A FAIR AND PROFESSIONAL MANNER, GIVING NO SPECIAL PREFERENCES OR ADVANTAGES TO ANY VENDOR.

• NEITHER SOLICIT NOR ACCEPT GRATUITIES OR OTHER FAVORS FROM VENDORS OR POTENTIAL VENDORS FOR YOU, YOUR SPOUSE, OR YOUR DEPENDENTS . THIS PROHIBITION DOES NOT INCLUDE ACCEPTING CALENDARS, DIARIES, OR OTHER PROMOTIONAL ARTICLES OF NOMINAL VALUE.

• REQUIRE OF VENDORS THE SAME HIGH QUALITY PRODUCT OR SERVICE AS WE OURSELVES PROVIDE.

EMPLOYEES ARE EXPECTED TO COMPLY WITH ALL REGULATIONS AND POLICIES RELATED TO THE USE OF COMPUTER SOFTWARE. COMPUTER SOFTWARE IS TO BE INSTALLED ONLY IN ACCORDANCE WITH LICENSING LAWS AND AGREEMENTS AND PERSONAL SOFTWARE MAY NOT BE USED ON COMPANY EQUIPMENT.

COMMUNITY AND GOVERNMENT RELATIONS

WE MUST ALL PARTICIPATE IN THE AFFAIRS OF OUR COMMUNITIES AND OUR GOVERNMENT TO ENSURE THEIR CONTINUED VIABILITY. CORPORATIONS AS WELL AS INDIVIDUALS MUST PLAY A ROLE. IN FULFILLING OUR RESPONSIBILITIES, WE SHOULD:

• BE RESPONSIBLE CITIZENS OF OUR LOCAL, STATE, AND NATIONAL COMMUNITIES.

• COMPLY WITH THE LAWS AND GOVERNMENT REGULATIONS AFFECTING OUR INDUSTRY AND OUR PERSONAL OBLIGATIONS. REALIZE THAT THE COMPANY WILL NOT TOLERATE OR CONDONE UNETHICAL OR UNLAWFUL ACTS. NO EXCUSE WILL BE ACCEPTED FOR ACTS THAT JEOPARDIZE THE GOODWILL AND REPUTATION OF THE COMPANY.

• BECOME INVOLVED IN CIVIC PROJECTS THAT CONTRIBUTE TO THE IMPROVEMENT OF OUR SOCIETY.

• PAY ALL TAX OBLIGATIONS COMPLETELY AND IN A TIMELY MANNER.

• BE CONCERNED WITH THE WELFARE OF OUR COMMUNITY.

• SUPPORT COMMUNITY PROGRAMS THAT BUILD CHARACTER AND INTEGRITY IN YOUNG PEOPLE.

• HELP THOSE LESS FORTUNATE THAN OURSELVES.

• ACT TO SAFEGUARD THE ENVIRONMENT.

• MAINTAIN OUR OFFICES AND HOMES TO MAKE THEM AESTHETIC ASSETS TO OURSELVES, OUR COMMUNITIES AND THE COMPANY.

• TAKE PART IN THE POLITICAL PROCESS BY EXERCISING OUR RIGHT TO SELECT OUR LEADERSHIP.

INDUSTRY COMMITMENT

WE BELIEVE THAT AS THE LEADING SECURITY SERVICE COMPANY WE HAVE A RESPONSIBILITY TO THE INDUSTRY AS A WHOLE. WE WANT TO BE AS PROUD OF THE INDUSTRY AS WE ARE OF OURSELVES. ACCORDINGLY, EACH OF US MUST:

• DEDICATE OURSELVES TO THE SAME STANDARDS OF EXCELLENCE THAT MAKE GUARDSMARK A PREMIER COMPANY IN ALL INDUSTRY.

• MAINTAIN A COMMITMENT TO THE IMPROVEMENT OF INDUSTRY STANDARDS, LEVELS OF PERFORMANCE, AND PUBLIC IMAGE.

• NOT RELY ON COMPETITORS' ACTIONS TO JUSTIFY OUR OWN ACTIONS. JUDGE OUR ACTIONS BY OUR OWN STANDARDS.

• MAINTAIN COMPETITIVE FAIRNESS BY NEITHER RECRUITING THE EMPLOYEES OF COMPETITORS NOR USING UNETHICAL TACTICS TO OBTAIN A COMPETITOR'S BUSINESS.

• NEVER ENGAGE IN ANTI-COMPETITIVE PRACTICES, FOR EXAMPLE, HAVING UNDERSTANDINGS, AGREEMENTS OR DISCUSSIONS WITH COMPETITORS CONCERNING PRICES, PRICING POLICIES, COSTS, BIDS OR OTHER POSSIBLE TERMS OF A POTENTIAL TRANSACTION.

• DO NOT OBTAIN INFORMATION REGARDING A COMPETITOR USING DECEPTIVE OR SURREPTITIOUS MEANS.

• NEVER SEEK OR UTILIZE CONFIDENTIAL OR PROPRIETARY INFORMATION OF A COMPETITOR.

• NEVER CRITICIZE A COMPETITOR. BEING BETTER THAN THE ORDINARY COMPANIES IS NOTHING EXCEPTIONAL; BEING BETTER THAN THE BEST COMPANIES IS THE GUARDSMARK STANDARD OF EXCELLENCE.

• RESPECT OUR PROFESSION. DO NOT DEMEAN IT BY WORD OR CONDUCT.

• BE PROFESSIONAL IN APPEARANCE AND IN PERFORMANCE OF OUR DUTIES.

• ACTIVELY PURSUE INNOVATIONS, CHANGES AND TECHNOLOGICAL IMPROVEMENTS THAT ENHANCE OUR ABILITY TO SERVICE OUR CLIENTS AND IMPROVE THE STATUS OF OUR PROFESSION.

PERSONAL COMMITMENT

BY SIGNING BELOW, EFFECTIVE TERRIFIC THURSDAY, AUGUST 28, 1996, WE AGREE TO ADHERE TO ALL STANDARDS STATED ABOVE DURING THE COURSE OF OUR AT-WILL EMPLOYMENT, AND WE FURTHERMORE BY OUR SIGNING ENCOURAGE EVERYONE TO JOIN OUR PLEDGE TO ADOPT PERSONAL STANDARDS OF INTEGRITY, RESPONSIBILITY, HONESTY, SELF-CONTROL, AND SELF-CONFIDENCE, AND OUR PLEDGE TO STRENGTHEN OUR WEAKNESSES AND BUILD ON OUR STRENGTHS. WE FURTHER ACCEPT THE RESPONSIBILITY OF INCORPORATING THE VALUES OF THIS CODE INTO OUR THOUGHTS AND ACTIONS EACH AND EVERY DAY. WE WILL LEAD BY EXAMPLE.

Our Code of Ethics is renewed annually by and for the employees of Guardsmark, Inc. It is effective on Thursday, August 28, 1996, and will be renewed on Thursday, August 29, 1997. If you need clarification of the principles of this Code or are in doubt about their application to a specific situation, please seek guidance from our Corporate Ethics Committee. They can reached at 1-800-238-5878 or 1-901-522-6000, or addressed at Guardsmark, Inc., P.O. Box 45, Memphis, Tennessee 38101-0045.

Commentary

This statement is more complete and directive than many of the others in this volume. Several stakeholders are mentioned—customers, employees, industry, vendors, community and government—and the company's as well as the employee's responsibility is well defined. The commitment to excellence section goes into substantial detail regarding each person's responsibility to contribute to this goal. The area of employee wellness is unique to this code and signifies the importance the company places on it. Personal commitment summarizes standards to which all employees should aspire. Two additional exemplary aspects of this document are its "sunset" provision with actual dates and the fact that nearly 100 managers sign off on the code annually, and then actual signatures are reprinted above the last paragraph.

A Halakhic Corporate Code of Ethics

General Provisions

Wealth: Each of us, as human beings, and as managers and employees, have a natural desire for wealth and profits, known as our yetzer (natural inclination), similar to our need for sex, food, and clothing. Although such needs are legitimate, they must operate within a certain moral framework. The goal is not to deprive one of the pursuit of wealth, nor of its fruits. The goal is to channel this yetzer into permitted and moral parameters so that this wealth may be kosher. The following code is an attempt to provide such a framework.

Tsedek and Chessed: Two central principles provide the foundation for all of our business activities: tsedek (fairness and justice), and chessed (goodness). In other words, one should follow not only the letter of the law, but the spirit of the law (lifnim mishurat hadin). God is, after all, not only King, but also Father.

Kiddush HaShem: Each time we deal with regulatory authorities, or with our customers, our suppliers, and our competitors, we have a great opportunity, and a tremendous challenge. We either act in such a manner so as to sanctify G-d's name (kiddush HaShem), or act in a manner which desecrates G-d's name (chillul HaShem).

Compliance with the Law: We are governed by the principle of dina d'malchuta dina (the law of the land must be followed, provided it does not contradict with Jewish law). We therefore must always ensure that our business activities are in compliance with the laws of whichever country we are operating in.

Abiding by Contracts: Although we may be legally entitled to sometimes default on some contractual agreements, we must always abide by any and all commitments, verbal or written, which we enter into. This should be the case even in situations where there appears to be no monetary loss to the other party or will cause financial loss to our firm.

Shareholders and Executive Officers

Lack of Corporate Veil: There does not seem to be a

corporate veil in Judaism, so that shareholders and directors are bound by all the moral restraints imposed by halakhic and spiritual teachings on the owners of wealth and their agents. Major shareholders are required to see that directors follow the code and dismiss them if they do not. Shareholders who because of their marginal holdings are unable to influence corporate policy would seem to be called upon to sell their stock in corporations that violated these teachings. Directors as agents of the shareholders are accountable for conducting the corporation according to its code of ethics. It is not humanly possible for managers and employees to adhere to the corporate code of ethics unless this code is made manifest by the behavior of the executive officer and supported by the shareholders.

Employees

Wages: This firm will pay its wages to its employees on the date set for such payment, without delay, otherwise we would be in breach of oshek (extortion). So, too, we will refrain from nonmonetary wages (perks, deferred remuneration, etc.) Where these are to the detriment of the employee.

Labor Policies: With respect to our labor policies, we will abide by any employment agreements entered into, local laws and local customers. although we are not obligated to guarantee job security for our employees, we are obligated to provide assistance to those employees who must be laid off, such as setting up an interest-free loan fund, or to assist them to establish their own business, or providing retraining. Decisions on lay-off priorities will be left to employees wherever possible. Our firm is obligated to provide severance pay, pensions, and partial employment or assistance to our aged workers who are no longer able to fulfill their job responsibilities. We are obligated to protect our workers against physical injury; this over and beyond the obligation to compensate them for work related illness. However, we, as acts of charity will share non-work related medical costs of long term employees with the employees and the public sector.

Theft: Employees will avoid engaging in all forms of theft including misuse of expense accounts, or the personal use of the firm's materials or facilities (e.g., long distance telephone, photocopier, fax machine). This applies also to the illegitimate use of computer software.

Insider Trading: Employees will not engage in insider trading. Where such a practice is forbidden by law, it is forbidden halakhically because of dina demalkhuta dina. In those countries where it is not legally forbidden, it is usually halakhically forbidden because of genevat da'at.

Bribes/Kickbacks: We will not receive or give any bribe, kickback or secret payments in our business activities. To do so would either be theft, or a violation of lifnei iver (blinding the eyes of the receiver).

Customers

Pricing: We will not charge customers for the goods we are selling or the services we are providing by any amount greater than its market value, unless customers are aware of the additional benefits they are receiving in paying a higher price. Care will be taken not to exploit any short-term difficulties encountered by our customers. To not act in this manner would be in breach of ona'ah (price oppression).

Selling Practices: Our firm does not accept the principle of "buyer beware." Instead, we will ensure that the buyer has accurate and full information regarding the nature and quality of the goods sold or services provided, without any concealment of defects or deficiencies. All goods sold or services provided will be according to those specified in the contract or as advertised. No products or services will be advertised which refer to instant gratification or unrealistic or exaggerated needs, or based on unsubstantiated claims. To do any of the above would be in violation of lifnei iver (putting a stumbling block in the path of the blind) or geneivat daat (stealing another's mind).

The firm will not sell goods or services that are harmful either physically or morally even in those cases where such sales are legal or done at the request and knowledge of the buyer.

Conflict of Interest: No advice will be given to customers or clients when the individual manager or employee giving the advice possesses a conflict of interest, without fully disclosing such interests. To do otherwise would be giving misleading advice, an aspect of lifnei iver.

Competitors

Competitive Practices: Although it is acceptable for our firm to enter new markets and compete with existing businesses, we will not do so if existing firms are faced with a total loss of their source of income. Our firm will not actively engage in the practice of luring employees from our competitors but will take rabbinic advice as to the circumstances under which this is permitted.

Suppliers

Obtaining Quotes: We will not obtain quotes from suppliers when we have no intention to buy from such a supplier. This would be in breach of verbal ona'ah (creating an expectation for a sale which when it doesn't materialize could cause mental anguish or represent a form of exploitation).

Repayment of Debts: We are obligated to fully repay our debts on time. We will take rabbinic advice as to the propriety of using debtor protection afforded by bankruptcy laws or provisions such as Chapter Eleven in the U.S.A.

Investors

Fraudulent Reporting: We will accurately represent all financial and accounting information. To do otherwise might encourage one to invest or conduct business with our firm based on inaccurate information, and would be in violation of geneivat da'at (stealing another's mind).

Community

Macro-Economic Policies: As part of our charitable obligations we will lobby for governmental policies that protect the poor, the aged, the sick and the marginal members of our society.

Environment: Our firm will do its utmost to respect the environment in which we operate. We are obligated to avoid polluting the water, air, or soil and to provide compensation for any damage which we may unintentionally cause.

Written by Mark Schwartz and Meir Tamari. The authors wish to express their thanks to Rabbis Baruch Taub, Aron Hoch, Amram Assayag and Breitowitz for their comments and insights.

Commentary

This code is grounded in the Jewish tradition. It begins with underlying religious principles and outlines corporate and managerial responsibilities to various stakeholders. It is a much more proactive code than most company ones and includes positive duties throughout the various sections—e.g., **Selling Practices**—*products will not be promoted to provide instant gratification and* **Macro-Economic Policies**—*lobby to assist the underprivileged members of society. Although the statement speaks directly to those of the Jewish faith, the message is one managers from all religious persuasions should contemplate.*

Hallmark Cards, Inc.

THIS IS HALLMARK

We believe:

That our *products and services* must enrich people's lives and enhance their relationships.

That *creativity and quality*—in our concepts, products and services—are essential to our success.

That the *people* of Hallmark are our company's most valuable resource.

That distinguished *financial performance* is a must, not as an end in itself, but as a means to accomplish our broader mission.

That our *private ownership* must be preserved.

The values that guide us are:

Excellence in all we do.

Ethical and moral conduct at all times and in all our relationships.

Innovation in all areas of our business as a means of attaining and sustaining leadership.

Corporate social responsibility to Kansas City and to each community in which we operate.

These beliefs and values guide our business strategies, our corporate behavior, and our relationships with suppliers, customers, communities and each other.

Commentary

These beliefs and values are used in lieu of a mission statement at Hallmark. The high level of aspiration of the firm is contained in the first belief statement. The ethical and moral conduct value is noteworthy not only for its inclusion, but also by the fact that "all" is used twice. It makes the point that ethical behavior is expected. The corporate home of Kansas City is specifically mentioned here. The above statement is presented to each employee in a greeting card format.

Although this document does not verbalize ethical principles as much as some others, the CEO Donald Hall remarked, "Our values are the only things that ultimately will protect us from making mistakes that would undermine our reputation, our integrity, and therefore, our success. Perhaps no other topic is a greater source of both pride and concern for me" (Jones and Kahaner, 1995).

Hanna Andersson

Our Purpose

In partnership with our customers, we will provide products to enhance the richly textured experience of family and community. We celebrate this experience through the integrity of our merchandise, and our respect for the values we share with our customers. Our culture bears witness to our beliefs.

Values

RESPECT

Recognizing and acknowledging the value and contribution of each person or endeavor. Acting with respect means treating others as you want to be treated.

INTEGRITY

Being true to your values and honest about your commitment to them.

RESPONSIBILITY

Being accountable for your actions and obligations, as a company and as individuals.

"Welcome to Hanna"

Ways to Grow and Participate

1. Be kind and intelligent with others, especially our customers. Respect, responsibility and integrity make good things happen.

---

2. Bring energy to your work. Big or small, if a task needs to be done, it needs to be done well. Think of each action in terms of how it strengthens Hanna.

3. Understand that learning prompts change. Together, they are the stepping stones to the evolution of our business.

4. Office politics take energy away from important work and divide rather than unite. It is work, and not talk, that matters.

5. When possible, plan your time off around the work flow. A balance between home life and Hanna is healthy and encouraged.

6. The Hanna environment should be clean, healthy and comfortable for everyone. Keep your work area organized and tidy. It is your job to pick up after yourself.

7. Your participation is encouraged. Learn as much as you can about your job, the company and our industry so that you may grow with us.

8. Hanna is sensitive to the actions and concerns of the community and the world around us. Avenues for social service and awareness are available to all.

9. We will all share in the success we create.

10. Laughter sees us through the day. Have fun.

Commentary

These three short statements outline the purpose, values and "Ten Commandments" of Hanna Andersson. The purpose makes reference to a number of ethical principles including partnership, integrity, shared values, and beliefs. The values statement was changed to include responsibility instead of fairness. Gun Denhart, Founder and CEO, explained: "We felt responsibility—fiscally and to the employees and customers—was a better word" (Jones and Kahaner 1995, 10). The ten ways to grow and participate reflect an environment that is caring, balanced and participative. The last one—have fun—lends a perspective that is often lacking in a corporate setting.

Herman Miller

OUR VALUES: WHO WE ARE

We value the diversity of individuals.

- We believe that diversity is fundamental to success; we rely on the contributions of men and women of diverse backgrounds, perspectives, ages, races, religions, cultures, and abilities.
- We believe in the integrity, dignity, and potential of every person.
- We believe that every individual's job is important and that all work can be rewarding and enjoyable.

We value ownership, participation, and teamwork.

- We believe that participation and teamwork are the best ways to manage a business.
- We believe that ownership is essential to participation.
- We believe that open and responsible communication among people at all levels is vital to success.
- We believe that managers best lead by serving.

We value excellence.

- We believe that striving to be the best—in our work, our relationships, our ideas, our facilities, and our practices—is the best demonstration of our commitment to customer satisfaction.
- We believe that integrity and accountability must never be compromised.
- We believe in celebration and recognition of work well done.

We value social and environmental responsibility.

- We believe that corporate policies and practices should be environmentally responsible and help individuals meet their responsibilities as members of families and communities.

We value learning, good design, and new ideas.

- We believe that research and good design can deliver superior products and services that solve problems to improve the quality of life.
- We believe that openness to change, innovation, risk, and failure is fundamental to our future success.
- We believe that there is always room to improve our results and competency through personal growth.

We value equity.

- We believe in equity for our customers, investors, vendors, dealers, and ourselves.
- We believe that excellent financial results must be earned and are essential to the future growth and vitality of our business.
- We believe that good stewardship of resources is everyone's responsibility.

OUR EXPECTATIONS: THE WAY WE WORK TOGETHER

- We expect personal integrity, competence, and commitment to excellence.
- We expect personal commitment to satisfying customers with superior quality and performance.
- We expect commitment to learning about the business and improving results.
- We expect opportunities for personal growth and responsibility for pursuing them.

We expect participation and accountability.

- We expect to be involved in the planning, organization, and control of our work and to take responsibility for its implementation.
- We expect our actions to demonstrate trust, respect for others, and a commitment to shared values and a common vision.
- We expect individuals and work teams to collaborate on resolution of cross functional issues.

■ We expect to be accountable and to hold others accountable for results.

■ We expect managers to be open, enabling, accessible, and empowering.

■ We expect management to make decisions that lead us toward our vision of excellence in all that we do and the way that we do it.

We expect equity for our investors, including ourselves.

Commentary

The values and expectations statements of Herman Miller make clear its guiding principles. Beginning each of the values statements with "We value . . ." and corresponding bullet points with "We believe..." and the expectations portion with "We expect . . ." gives the strong impression that they will be followed. These statements empha-size the importance of individuals as persons who are working toward a common goal. Certain words such as "integrity," "openness," "ac-countability" and "responsiblity" are repeated in several places to show their importance and pervasiveness. Both the expectations of management and employees are well articulated here. These statements are an outgrowth of Herman Miller's philosophy developed over sev-eral CEOs, the most noteworthy being Max DePree (1989; 1992), whose uplifting writings stressed leadership, stewardship and ethical behavior.

Hershey Foods

Guidelines for Ethical Business Practices

RELATIONSHIPS WITH CUSTOMERS AND SUPPLIERS

Hershey Foods recognizes that normal business practice and common courtesy sometimes require that gifts, favors and entertainment be extended to present or prospective customers, or be received from present or prospective suppliers. These occasions, however, must be strictly limited and carefully defined. There is never an occasion for secret commissions, hidden gratuities or payments to anyone who might have influence on customers, suppliers or officials.

There are certain guidelines and conditions that must be followed to assure compliance with the Key Corporate Policies. The guidelines and conditions are:

1. <u>GIFTS, FAVORS AND ENTERTAINMENT</u>

Employees should use good judgment and common sense in offering or accepting business gifts, favors or entertainment. A single, modest lunch may have no influence on a business decision. Accepting or offering free meals on a regular basis may have a different effect. At the very least, it may create a perception of misconduct.

Therefore, only if **all** of the following criteria are met, may any Hershey Foods employee extend personal gifts, favors or entertainment to any customer, potential customer or receive same from any supplier:

- They are not in violation of any applicable law or regulation.

- They are not offered or received directly or indirectly in exchange for a specific gain or action.

- They are in keeping with the generally accepted ethical standards of the country where the action takes place.

- They are in such form that they cannot be construed as a bribe, payoff or deal.

- Public disclosure of the facts surrounding them would not embarrass the Corporation or those giving/receiving the gift, favor or entertainment.

And, depending on the circumstances, one of the next two criteria are also complied with:

- They are gifts worth less than $25 in value and typically are of an advertising or promotional nature. Depending upon the circumstances, gifts or favors in excess of $25 may be accepted <u>only</u> if approved by the employee's manager; or

- They are common social amenities normally associated with accepted business practice, such as lunches and dinners. Amenities of this nature, even if they exceed $25, are within the employee's purview to offer or accept. However, amenities that go beyond normal or common business practice must be approved by the employee's manager or beyond if deemed necessary.

The above is not intended to overly restrict participation in business-related functions and activities, such as lunches, dinners and entertainment. These can be, under proper circumstances, in the best interests of the Corporation. Customary acts of hospitality to an employee or representative of a customer, such as the purchase of meals, are permissible if not contrary to the above criteria and if reported under standard expense account procedures. Such acts, however, shall be of such a nature so as to avoid any question of impropriety by the Corporation or the recipient of the hospitality. When in doubt about a particular action or situation, employees should always seek additional guidance from their manager first and subsequently a higher level if necessary.

2. <u>TRIPS AND OUTINGS - BUSINESS AND PLEASURE</u>

It is entirely proper to invite Hershey Foods customers, both present and prospective, or to be invited by suppliers on trips/outings so long as the purpose, conduct and projected expenses meet all of the aforementioned guidelines and conditions and the necessary approval(s) has been granted.

Special invitations to hunting, fishing, golfing or similar trips which may be expensive can tend to create feelings of obligation that are contrary to their intent. Under certain circumstances, however, such activities would be in the best interests of the Corporation and contribute to good working relationships with customers and suppliers. Before offering or accepting any invitation of this type, employees must seek the approval of their manager, who in turn may deem it necessary to seek a higher level of approval depending on the extent of the expenditure involved. If it is agreed that attendance at such a function will serve a useful business purpose, the invitation may be accepted or extended.

Additional guidance can be drawn from the following:

Business trips - such as facility visits - are considered totally appropriate as a means of maintaining goodwill and of trying to influence a customer into taking a specific action. Payment of all expenses, as well as business-related gifts (of limited nominal value) as a memento of the occasion, are all well within the bounds of accepted business practice.

Pleasure trips and outings - for customers and suppliers are proper when they are intended to create or maintain goodwill. Examples include a trip to a sporting event, a day at the golf course, or attendance at a cultural event. These kinds of trips are not permissible when they are intended to influence a specific customer action. In other words, you can't take a customer to a Super Bowl game and suggest that the customer repay the favor with a specific business action favorable to Hershey Foods. This type of "leverage" entertainment goes against corporate policy.

Dual purpose trips - when a trip is for more than one purpose, but includes pleasure, it must conform to the restrictions placed upon pleasure trips and outings.

3. PAYMENT TO EXPEDITE OR FACILITATE SERVICE

In a number of foreign countries, tips and gratuities of a minor nature are customarily required by low-level governmental representatives performing administrative or clerical duties to secure the timely and correct completion of their responsibilities. Examples include customs clearance, visa applications and exchange transactions.

Where payments of this nature are unavoidable, they may be made only to facilitate the correct performance of the government representative's routine duties. Payments may not be made to induce foreign officials to fail to perform their duties or to perform them in an incorrect manner.

CRITERIA FOR ETHICAL DECISIONS

The following criteria for ethical decision making can be applied to any act or situation to help employees comply with the Corporation's expectations for proper business conduct:

- Is anyone's life, health or safety endangered by the action?

- Is the action legal? If legal, is it ethical?

- Does the action comply with established policy or approved practice?

- Will this act be handled honestly and openly in every respect?

- Would the employee be compromised or embarrassed if this act were known by his/her boss, fellow employees, subordinates, or friends?

- Does the intended action have the appearance of an inappropriate act or course of behavior?

- Does the employee feel uncomfortable about doing the act?

- Should the employee ask his/her supervisor about this act before taking action?

Commentary

These three sections of Hershey's Guidelines for Ethical Business Practices spell out the expectations regarding the company's relationship with customers and suppliers. The giving and receiving of gifts, trips and outings, and facilitating payments represent potentially troublesome areas for most firms. Hershey has provided concrete guidance to its employees and specific cases are posed and analyzed in the Guidelines booklet. The section above on the criteria for ethical decisions is included at the end and asks several substantive questions for the employee to ponder.

Hewlett Packard

The HP Way
Organizational Values
HP's values are a set of deeply held beliefs that govern and guide our behavior in meeting our objectives and in dealing with each other, our customers, shareholders and others.

⇔ **We have trust and respect for individuals.** We approach each situation with the understanding that people want to do a good job and will do so, given the proper tools and support. We attract highly capable, innovative people and recognize their efforts and contributions to the company. HP people contribute enthusiastically and share in the success that they make possible.

⇔ **We focus on a high level of achievement and contribution.** Our customers expect HP products and services to be of the highest quality and to provide lasting value. To achieve this, all HP people, but especially managers, must be leaders who generate enthusiasm and respond with extra effort to meet customer needs. Techniques and management practices which are effective today may be outdated in the future. For us to remain at the forefront in all our activities, people should always be looking for new and better ways to do their work.

⇔ **We conduct our business with uncompromising integrity.** We expect HP people to be open and honest in their dealings to earn the trust and loyalty of others. People at every level are expected to adhere to the highest standards of business ethics and must understand that anything less is totally unacceptable. As a practical matter, ethical conduct cannot be assured by written HP policies and codes; it must be an integral part of the organization, a deeply ingrained tradition that is passed from one generation of employees to another.

⇔ **We achieve our common objectives through teamwork.** We recognize that it is only through effective cooperation within and among organizations that we can achieve our goals. Our commitment is to work as a worldwide team to fulfill the expectations of our customers, shareholders and others who

---

depend upon us. The benefits and obligations of doing business are shared among all HP people.

⇔ **We encourage flexibility and innovation.** We create a work environment which supports the diversity of our people and their ideas. We strive for overall objectives which are clearly stated and agreed upon, and allow people flexibility in working toward goals in ways which they help determine are best for the organization. HP people should personally accept responsibility and be encouraged to upgrade their skills and capabilities through ongoing training and development. This is especially important in a technical business where the rate of progress is rapid and where people are expected to adapt to change.

Commentary

The HP Way was developed by William Hewlett and David Packard in the early days of their firm. The five values show a visionary sense of the importance of people, ingenuity and ethical practice. These values still serve as the guiding set of principles for the firm. The statement was highlighted in obituaries of David Packard in 1996. One stated: "The deep respect and concern for employees they called 'the HP Way' now is synonymous with corporate integrity" (Hamilton 1996). Developing and living by the HP Way distinguishes this company from most others.

Hong Kong Ethics Development Centre

STANDARDS OF BEHAVIOUR

It is up to each individual business organisation to determine the ethical standards of behaviour of its management and employees. The common approach is to take into account legal requirements, a company's own ethical values and general community expectations.

Compliance with Law . . .

Obviously, abiding by the law has to be an absolutely vital part of a code of conduct.

Collective Standards of Practice . . .

There already exist established standards of practice governing collectively the conduct of listed companies on the stock exchange, specific trades and professions as well as special types of business corporations.

Basic Values . . .

Ethical behaviour is behaviour which goes beyond legal requirements. It essentially comes down to honesty, equity, integrity and social responsibilities. These are the basic values for resolving difficult legal and ethical questions.

Ethics Test . . .

It is not possible to prescribe exhaustive guidelines to cover each and every single ethical concern that employees are likely to face in their work. When in doubt, **the test is whether or not it would survive disclosure and critical public scrutiny.** A breach of business ethics thus may extend beyond a violation of legal requirements.

Commentary

This is a different type of ethics document. The Hong Kong Ethics Development Center was formed under the auspices of the Community

---

Relations Department of the Independent Commission Against Corruption. It works with companies to develop codes, control systems and staff training to implement ethics into their organizations. These four standards indicate to companies the areas upon which they should focus in developing such statements and programs. The Ethics Test section makes a telling point that these documents cannot be exhaustive, but the boldface comment provides an excellent decision rule to use.

Hormel Food Corporation

Company Values

Our mission will be accomplished by focusing on values relating to our consumers, customers, employees, shareholders, suppliers and the communities we serve.

Consumers—We strive to:
⇔ anticipate, listen and respond to consumer desires for innovative new products.
⇔ develop loyal consumers through continuous improvement of product quality and consistency.
⇔ be a trustworthy provider of wholesome, nutritious and good tasting food products of excellent value.

Trade Customers—We strive to:
⇔ provide service that is innovative, responsive, reliable, courteous and professional.
⇔ develop partnerships with our customers to assure mutual success.
⇔ provide quality products supported by innovative and effective marketing programs.

Employees—We seek to provide an environment in which:
⇔ all employees trust and respect one another.
⇔ teamwork and positive attitudes are commonplace.
⇔ all ideas are valued, respected and recognized.
⇔ continuous improvement, innovation and prevention are a way of life.
⇔ everyone strives to satisfy customers at all times.

Shareholders—We are committed to:
⇔ long-term profitability and growth.
⇔ providing optimum economic value for our shareholders.
⇔ a satisfactory return on assets employed.
⇔ making sound economic decisions based on thorough risk and return assessments.

Suppliers—We develop mutually beneficial supplier relationships built on:

⇔ trust and respect.

⇔ optimization of total value through innovation, technology, and process involvement.

⇔ quality, price and service.

Communities—We serve our communities by:

⇔ operating modern, clean, safe and efficient facilities which add value to the community.

⇔ our active participation and leadership in community affairs.

⇔ leading and supporting community and national efforts to improve the environment.

Commentary

This values statement spells out Hormel's commitments to six stakeholder groups. Two types of consumers are specified and come first. The importance of trust to consumers, employees and suppliers is noted. Quality and continuous improvement is a theme in several stakeholder statements. This document focuses both on business and ethical/social values and does it in an effective manner.

Hyatt

Discrimination Policy

Hyatt is committed to providing a work environment that is free of discrimination. In keeping with this commitment, we maintain a strict policy prohibiting unlawful harassment, including sexual harassment. This policy applies to all employees of Hyatt, including supervisors and non-supervisory employees. It prohibits harassment in any form, including verbal and physical harassment.

Sexual harassment is a behavior which undermines the integrity of the employment relationship. All employees must be allowed to work in an environment free from unsolicited and unwelcome sexual overtures. Sexual harassment does not refer to occasional compliments. It refers to behavior which is not welcome, which is personally offensive, which reduces morale, and which therefore interferes with employee effectiveness.

Sexual harassment may include actions such as:

1 Unwelcomed or unwanted sexual advances. This could include any form of physical contact.

2 Requests or demands for sexual favors. This could include subtle or blatant expectations. It also includes pressure or requests for any type of sexual favor accompanied by an implied or stated promise or preferential treatment or negative consequences concerning any aspect of one's employment status.

Hyatt
Corporate
Discrimination
Policy

3 Verbal abuse. Conversation that is sexually-oriented and that may be expected to be unacceptable to another individual. This could include inappropriate comments about an individual's body or appearance where such comments go beyond a mere compliment; telling "dirty jokes" that may be expected to be offensive; or any other tasteless, sexually-oriented comments, innuendoes or actions that offend others.

4 Engaging in any type of sexually-oriented conduct that interferes with another's work performance or the work environment. This includes extending unwanted sexual attention to someone.

5 Creating a work environment that is intimidating, hostile or offensive because of sexually-oriented conversation, suggestions, requests, demands, physical contacts or attention.

Normal, pleasant, courteous, mutually respectful and non-coercive interaction between employees is **not** considered to be sexual harassment. However, sexual harassment is an insidious practice which demeans individuals being treated in such a manner. Hyatt will not tolerate sexual harassment of its employees by anyone—supervisors, employees, clients and/or customers. Employees who violate this policy are subject to termination.

Reprint is used courtesy of Hyatt Hotels Corporation.

Commentary

This plain-speaking statement is one of the best corporate positions on the difficult issue of sexual harassment. Hyatt's Corporate Discrimination Policy is contained within the company ethics statement. A seventeen-point policy statement precedes the discrimination one, but these are relatively brief. Placing specific emphasis on discrimination and harassment sends a strong signal to employees and other stakeholders that Hyatt takes this issue very seriously. The five points go well beyond the EEOC interpretation of what constitutes this practice.

Johnson & Johnson

Our Credo

We believe our first responsibility is to the doctors, nurses and patients, to mothers and fathers and all others who use our products and services.

In meeting their needs everything we do must be of high quality.

We must constantly strive to reduce our costs in order to maintain reasonable prices.

Customers' orders must be serviced promptly and accurately.

Our suppliers and distributors must have an opportunity to make a fair profit.

We are responsible to our employees, the men and women who work with us throughout the world.

Everyone must be considered as an individual.

We must respect their dignity and recognize their merit.

They must have a sense of security in their jobs.

Compensation must be fair and adequate, and working conditions clean, orderly and safe.

We must be mindful of ways to help our employees fulfill their family responsibilities.

Employees must feel free to make suggestions and complaints.

There must be equal opportunity for employment, development and advancement for those qualified.

We must provide competent management, and their actions must be just and ethical.

We are responsible to the communities in which we live and work and to the world community as well.

We must be good citizens—support good works and charities and bear our fair share of taxes.

We must encourage civic improvements and better health and education.

We must maintain in good order the property we are privileged
to use, protecting the environment and natural resources.

Our final responsibility is to our stockholders.

Business must make a sound profit.

We must experiment with new ideas.

Research must be carried on, innovative programs developed
and mistakes paid for.

New equipment must be purchased, new facilities provided and
new products launched.

Reserves must be created to provide for adverse times.

When we operate according to these principles, the stockholders
should realize a fair return.

Commentary

*The J&J credo is probably the best known ethics statement in the
world, at least partially due to the central role it played in the tragic
Tylenol poisonings. Not as well known is the fact that J&J has trans-
lated the credo into many languages and is conspicuously displayed in
company offices worldwide. For example, when I interviewed the
Managing Director of a J&J subsidiary (Janssen Pharmaceuticals) in
Ireland, the enlarged credo hung both in the waiting area and outside
the MD's office. The order of the four paragraphs is purposeful in that
stockholders are intentionally listed last. J&J's view is that if the
responsibilities to the other stakeholders are fulfilled, the stockholders
will earn a fair return. Another important aspect of the credo is that
the company conducts surveys with its employees biannually to determine the impact of the credo on day-to-day activities. For more information about the credo, see Murphy (1989), Nash (1988) and Williams
and Murphy (1990).*

Johnson Controls, Inc.

Johnson Controls Vision

OUR CREED

We believe in the free enterprise system. We shall consistently treat our customers, employees, shareholders, suppliers and the community with honesty, dignity, fairness and respect. We will conduct our business with the highest ethical standards.

OUR MISSION

Continually exceed our customers' increasing expectations.

WHAT WE VALUE

INTEGRITY: Honesty and fairness are essential to the way we do business and how we interact with people. We are a company that keeps its promises. We do what we say we will do, and we will conduct ourselves in accordance with our code of ethics.

CUSTOMER SATISFACTION: Customer satisfaction is the source of employee, shareholder, supplier and community benefits. We will exceed customer expectations through continuous improvements in quality, service, productivity, and time compression.

OUR EMPLOYEES: The diversity and involvement of our people is the foundation of our strength. We are committed to their fair and effective selection, development, motivation and recognition. We will provide employees with the tools, training and support to achieve excellence in customer satisfaction.

IMPROVEMENT AND INNOVATION: We seek improvement and innovation in every element of our business.

SAFETY AND ENVIRONMENT: Our products, services and workplaces reflect our belief that what is good for the environment and the safety and health of all people is good for Johnson Controls.

Commentary

Johnson Controls' Vision encompasses three separate elements. First, the creed specifies clearly the emphasis on ethics in the treatment

---

of the various stakeholders. The mission is short, but it is stated that the company wants to "exceed" rather than just meet customer expectations. The values portion begins with the essential ingredient of integrity. Employees and customers also merit individual discussion in the values statement as well. A unique value is the one on improvement and innovation, but it follows logically from the mission noted above.

Kroger

OUR MISSION is to be a leader in the distribution and merchandising of food, health, personal care, and related consumable products and services. In achieving this objective, we will satisfy our responsibilities to shareowners, employees, customers, suppliers, and the communities we serve.

We will conduct our business to produce financial returns that reward investment by shareholders and allow the company to grow. Investments in retailing, distribution and food processing will be continually evaluated for their contribution to our corporate objectives.

We will constantly strive to satisfy consumer needs better than the best of our competitors. Operating procedures will reflect our beliefs that the organizational levels closest to the consumer are best positioned to respond to changing consumer needs.

We will treat our employees fairly and with respect, openness and honesty. We will solicit and respond to their ideas and reward meaningful contributions to our success.

We value America's diversity and will strive to reflect that diversity in our work force, the companies with whom we do business, and the customers we serve. As a company, we will convey respect and dignity to each individual.

We will encourage our employees to be active, responsible citizens and will allocate resources for activities that enhance the quality of life for our customers, our employees and the communities we serve.

(Joseph A. Pichler CEO)

Commentary

Although this statement is labeled as a mission, it contains elements of a values and ethics type document too. The employee section makes reference to moral values and the diversity point is made clearly. The statement also has a strong stakeholder flavor to it. In a speech, Mr. Pichler discussed how he tries to create a moral corporate culture at Kroger. Some of his points were to enforce the code, be fair with violators, listen carefully and give employees a sense of ownership (Laczniak and Murphy 1993, 300).

LEGO

The 10 LEGO Rules

1. Be objective and truthful

2. Be positive and unpretentious

3. Be economical

4. Be international

5. Evoke enthusiasm and inspire

6. Encourage imagination and activity

7. Observe characteristics

8. Take precedence of sublimate self

9. Always finish the job

10. Follow company policy

The 10 LEGO Characteristics

LEGO
1. unlimited play possibilities

LEGO
2. for girls, for boys

LEGO
3. enthusiasm for all ages

LEGO
4. play for all year round

LEGO
5. stimulating and harmonious play

LEGO
6. endless hours of play

LEGO
7. imagination, creativity, development

LEGO
8. each new product multiplies the play value

LEGO
9. always topical

LEGO
10. safety and quality

Commentary

LEGO means "play well" and the company has attempted to live true to its name. Though these statements are rather terse, they do signal a commitment to children and corporate ethical behavior. The order appears to be significant in that the first LEGO rule is to be objective and truthful while the last is to "follow company policy." In other words, truth always wins out over company politics. The other rules give brief guidance to employees and their short nature can probably be attributed to the company headquarters being located in the Scandinavian country of Denmark. Although the ten characteristics are more product related, the last one notes the importance of safety and quality. This area receives special emphasis because the product safety committee at LEGO reports directly to the CEO.

Levi Strauss & Co.

Aspirations Statement

We all want a Company that our people are proud of and committed to, where all employees have an opportunity to contribute, learn, grow and advance based on merit, not politics or background. We want our people to feel respected, treated fairly, listened to and involved. Above all, we want satisfaction from accomplishments and friendships, balanced personal and professional lives, and to have fun in our endeavors.

When we describe the kind of LS&CO. we want in the future what we are talking about is building on the foundation we have inherited: affirming the best of our Company's traditions, closing gaps that may exist between principle and practices and updating some of our values to reflect contemporary circumstances.

What type of leadership is necessary to make our Aspirations a reality?

TEAMWORK AND TRUST: Leadership that exemplifies directness, openness to influence, commitment to the success of others, willingness to acknowledge our own contributions to problems, personal accountability, teamwork and trust. Not only must we model these behaviors but we must coach others to adopt them.	DIVERSITY: Leadership that values a diverse workforce (age, sex, ethnic group, etc.) at all levels of the organization, diversity in experience and a diversity in perspectives. We have committed to taking full advantage of the rich backgrounds and abilities of all our people and to promote a greater diversity in positions of influence. Differing points of view will be sought; diversity will be valued and honesty rewarded, not suppressed.

RECOGNITION: Leadership that provides greater recognition—both financial and psychic—for individuals and teams that contribute to our success. Recognition must be given to all who contribute: those who create and innovate and also those who continually support the day-to-day business requirements.

ETHICAL MANAGEMENT PRACTICES: Leadership that epitomizes the stated standards of ethical behavior. We must provide clarity about our expectations and must enforce these standards throughout the corporation.

COMMUNICATIONS: Internally, leadership that builds an environment where information is actively shared, sought and used in ways that lead to empowerment that works, improved performance, and meaningful feedback. Externally, leadership that strengthens our corporate reputation with key stakeholders. All communications should be clear, timely and honest.

EMPOWERMENT: Leadership that promotes ways of working in which responsibility, authority and accountability for decision making are held by those closest to our products and customers, and every employee has the necessary perspective, skills and knowledge to be successful in his or her job. We all share responsibility for creating the environment that will nurture empowerment at all levels of the organization.

Code of Ethics

Levi Strauss & Co. has a long and distinguished history of ethical conduct and community involvement. Essentially, these are a reflection of the mutually shared values of the founding families and of our employees.

OUR ETHICAL VALUES ARE BASED ON THE FOLLOWING ELEMENTS:

- A commitment to commercial success in terms broader than

merely financial measures.

- A respect for our employees, suppliers, customers, consumers and stockholders.
- A commitment to conduct which is not only legal but fair and morally correct in a fundamental sense.
- Avoidance of not only real, but the appearance of conflict of interest.

From time to time the Company will publish specific guidelines, policies and procedures. However, the best test of whether something is ethically correct is whether you would be prepared to present it to our senior management and board of directors as being consistent with our ethical traditions. If you have any uneasiness about an action you are about to take or which you see, you should discuss the action with your supervisor or management.

Ethical Principles

Our ethical principles are the values that set the ground rules for all that we do as employees of Levi Strauss & Co. As we seek to achieve responsible commercial success, we will be challenged to balance these principles against each other, always mindful of our promise to shareholders that we will achieve responsible commercial success.

The Ethical Principles Are:

HONESTY We will not say things that are false. We will never deliberately mislead. We will be as candid as possible, openly and freely sharing information, as appropriate to the relationship.

PROMISE-KEEPING We will go to great lengths to keep our commitments. We will not make promises that can't be kept and we will not make promises on behalf of the Company unless we have the authority to do so.

FAIRNESS We will create and follow a process and achieve outcomes that a reasonable person would call just, evenhanded and nonarbirtrary.

RESPECT FOR OTHERS We will create and direct in our communication, and receptive to influence. We will honor and value the abilities and contributions of others, embracing the responsibility and accountability for our actions in this regard.

COMPASSION We will maintain an awareness of the needs of others and act to meet those need whenever possible. We will also minimize harm whenever possible. We will act in ways that are consistent with our commitment to social responsibility.

INTEGRITY We will live up to LS&CO.'s ethical principles; even when confronted by personal, professional and social risks, as well as economic pressures.

Global Sourcing & Operating Guidelines

Levi Strauss & Co. seeks to conduct its business in a responsible manner. In 1991, Levi Strauss & Co. was the first multinational company to establish comprehensive Global Sourcing & Operating Guidelines.

Business Partners

Our Global Sourcing & Operating Guidelines help us to select business partners who follow work place standards and business practices that are consistent with our company's policies. These requirements are applied to every contractor who manufactures or finishes products for Levi Strauss & Co. Trained inspectors closely audit and monitor compliance among approximately 500 cutting, sewing, and finishing contractors in more than 50 countries.

Partnerships That Work

For Levi Strauss & Co., implementing our guidelines is a comprehensive and resource-intensive effort. Our goal is to achieve positive results and effect change not to punish contractors for transgressions. Through our guidelines, we seek long-term solutions that will benefit the individuals who make our products and will improve the quality of life in the communities in which they live.

In Bangladesh, our initial Terms of Engagement evaluations revealed that several underage girls were working in two contractors' facilities. Rather than dismiss the girls, which would have put them at risk of exploitation and economic hardship,

Levi Strauss & Co. teamed up with the contractors to develop an innovative solution. The contractors agreed to stop employing underage workers, and to continue to pay a salary to the girls, provided that they attend school. Levi Strauss & Co. paid for tuition, books, and school uniforms for the girls. The contractors, in turn, pledged jobs for the girls after completion of their schooling.

The Levi Strauss & Co. Sourcing & Operating Guidelines include two parts:

I.   The Business Partner Terms of Engagement, which deal with issues that are substantially controllable by Levi Strauss & Co.'s individual business partners.

II.   The Country Assessment Guidelines, which address larger, external issues beyond the control of individual business partners (e.g., health and safety issues and political, economic, and social conditions). These help us assess the risk of doing business in a particular country.

These standards are an integral part of our business. Company employees have the authority and the responsibility to take any steps necessary to ensure compliance with all standards and policies. Our employees and business partners understand that our guidelines are no less important than meeting our quality standards or delivery times.

In Pereira, Colombia, Levi Strauss & Co. worked with a contractor to redesign factory floor space, improve access to exits, and develop an effective emergency preparedness and evacuation plan. Several weeks after these improvements had been made, Pereira was rocked by a severe earthquake. Amidst extensive damage and injury to surrounding buildings and workers, all of our contractor's employees were able to safely exit the factory. The changes initiated under our Terms of Engagement policies are credited with preventing injury or death to the workers at this factory.

As a result of LS&CO.-contractor alliances, more than 35 water treatment systems have been built or upgraded at laundry and product finishing centers in countries such as Morocco, Thailand, Mexico, Brazil, Philippines, Guatemala and Pakistan. Many of these facilities have incorporated innovative programs to recycle treated water. For example, at one of our contracted laundries in El Paso, Texas, treated water is used to irrigate an adjacent field.

Terms of Engagement
1. Ethical Standards
We will seek to identify and utilize business partners who aspire as individuals and in the conduct of all their businesses to a set of ethical standards not incompatible with our own.

2. Legal Requirements
We expect our business partners to be law abiding as individuals and to comply with legal requirements relevant to the conduct of all their businesses.

3. Environmental Requirements
We will only do business with partners who share our commitment to the environment and who conduct their business in a way that is consistent with Levi Strauss & Co.'s Environmental Philosophy and Guiding Principles.

4. Community Involvement
We favor business partners who share our commitment to contribute to improving community conditions.

5. Employment Standards
We will only do business with partners whose workers are in all cases present voluntarily, not put at risk of physical harm, fairly compensated, allowed the right of free association and not exploited in any way. In addition, the following specific guidelines will be followed:

Wages and Benefits: We will only do business with partners who provide wages and benefits that comply with any applicable law and match the prevailing local manufacturing or finishing industry practices.

In Puerto Rico, a Levi Strauss & Co. contractor was the first on the island to retrofit factories with facilities accessible to the disabled. In these same three plants, doctors hold open office hours five days-a-week to treat families of employees. Through a contractor/LS&CO. alliance, the factories also sponsor summer work programs to help pay the college tuition of employees and their families.

Since the establishment of our Global Sourcing & Operating Guidelines, we have witnessed significant growth in community involvement programs sponsored by our business partners. In a small town in Mexico, one of our contractors started a program that purchases books and other school supplies for students' costs which in the past limited basic education opportunities to children from wealthier families. As a result of this program, the overall education standards and level of school attendance has increased notably for all children in the community.

Working Hours: While permitting flexibility in scheduling, we will identify prevailing local work hours and seek business partners who do not exceed them except for appropriately compensated overtime. While we favor partners who utilize less than sixty-hour work weeks, we will not use contractors who, on a regular basis, require in excess of a sixty-hour week. Employees should be allowed at least one day off in seven.

Child Labor: Use of child labor is not permissible. Workers can be no less than 14 years of age and not younger than the compulsory age to be in school. We will not utilize partners who use child labor in any of their facilities. We support the development of legitimate workplace apprenticeship programs for the educational benefit of younger people.

Prison Labor/Forced Labor: We will not utilize prison or forced labor in contracting relationships in the manufacture and finishing of our products. We will not utilize or purchase materials from a business partner utilizing prison or forced labor.

Health & Safety: We will only utilize business partners who provide workers with a safe and healthy work environment. Business partners who provide residential facilities for their workers must provide safe and healthy facilities.

Discrimination: While we recognize and respect cultural differences, we believe that workers should be employed on the basis of their ability to do the job, rather than on the basis of personal characteristics or beliefs. We will favor business partners who share this value.

Disciplinary Practices: We will not utilize business partners who use corporal punishment or other forms of mental or physical coercion.

In Indonesia, our contractors have implemented changes to improve the health, safety, and workplace conditions for their employees. These changes include: production line redesigns that have reduced crowding and improved efficiency; improvements to ventilation systems; construction of new chemical storage systems; electrical wiring and lighting retrofits; the codification and enforcement of workers' rights; and increased wages and benefits.

In response to a recommendation made during a Terms of Engagement evaluation, one of our business partners in Tunisia designed and implemented a program to promote worker diversity at sewing factories that have traditionally employed only women. In partnership with the Government of Tunisia, the contractor established an innovative job training program to create new opportunities for young men, including those with disabilities. Graduates of the program are qualified to hold skilled positions in a sewing factory. The contractor has been recognized in the community as an innovative employer actively encouraging diversity in the workplace and supporting the productive employment of disabled workers.

Evaluation & Compliance

All new and existing factories involved in the cutting, sewing, or finishing of products for Levi Strauss & Co. must comply with our Terms of Engagement. These facilities are continuously evaluated to ensure compliance. We work on-site with our contractors to develop strong alliances dedicated to responsible business practices and continuous improvement.

If Levi Strauss & Co. determines that a business partner is in violation of our Terms of Engagement, the company may withdraw production from that factory or require that a contractor implement a corrective action plan within a specified time period. If a contractor fails to meet the corrective action plan commitment, Levi Strauss & Co. will terminate the business relationship.

Our Commitment

Levi Strauss & Co. is committed to continuous improvement in the implementation of our Global Sourcing & Operating Guidelines. As these standards are applied throughout the world, we will continue to take into consideration all pertinent information that helps us better address issues of concern, meet new challenges, and improve our guidelines.

Country Assessment Guidelines

The diverse cultural, social, political, and economic circumstances of the various countries where Levi Strauss & Co. has existing or future business interests raise issues that could subject our coporate reputation and therefore, our business success, to potential harm. The Country Assessment Guidelines are intended to help us assess these issues. The Guidelines are tools that assist us in making practical and principled business decisions as we balance the potential risks and opportunities associated with conducting business in a particular country.

In making these decisions, we consider the degree to which our global corporate reputation and commercial success may be exposed to unreasonable risk. Specifically we assess whether the:

BRAND IMAGE would be adversely affected by a country's perception or image among our customers and/or consumers;

HEALTH AND SAFETY of our employees and their families, or our Company representatives would be exposed to unreasonable risk.

HUMAN RIGHTS ENVIRONMENT would prevent us from conducting business activities in a manner that is consistent with the Global Sourcing Guidelines and other Company policies;

LEGAL SYSTEM would prevent us from adequately protecting our trademarks, investments or other commercial interests, or from implementing the Global Sourcing Guidelines and other Company policies; and

POLITICAL, ECONOMIC AND SOCIAL ENVIRONMENT would threaten the Company's reputation and/or commercial interests.

In making these assessments, we take into account the various types of business activities and objectives proposed (e.g. procurement of fabric and sundries, sourcing, licensing, direct investments in subsidiaries) and, thus, the accompanying level of risk involved.

Commentary

Several Levi Strauss & Co. (LS&CO.) ethics statements are reprinted here. The title of the first one—the aspirations statement—

---

seems to be significant because management realizes that they and their employees can always improve. The focus on leadership in the six areas is noteworthy. Management is acutely aware of its critical responsibility by indicating executives should "epitomize" the company's stated ethical standards. The code and principles statements emphasize the underlying values pervading LS&CO. The value of "compassion" is unique. The final documents shown above guide LS&CO.'s international operations. The company has received much favorable coverage on their business partner relationships and the guidelines for country selection (Katz and Paine 1995; Mitchell 1994). LS&CO. has taken an international leadership role in following through on these policies, especially regarding its decision not to do business in China in 1993 (Jones and Kahaner 1995), and is viewed in some circles as the best example of effective implementation of corporate ethical policies in the 1990s.

Marriott

Ethical Conduct Policy

Marriott International conducts business with uncompromising ethical standards. Adherence to such standards should never be traded in favor of financial or other business objectives. High ethical standards are necessary to maintain our competitive advantage, earn the confidence of our associates and to provide quality products and services to customers and clients.

The company expects every associate to follow high ethical standards and promote ethical behavior. Associates should avoid seeking loopholes, shortcuts or technicalities and should reject the notion that unethical behavior is acceptable because "everyone is doing it." You should judge every action by considering whether it is legal, fair to all concerned and able to withstand the scrutiny of outsiders. Associates whose behavior is found to violate ethical standards will be subject to disciplinary action including, where appropriate, termination.

In order for the Company to conduct business with high ethical standards, every Marriott associate will:

Obey all relevant laws, including those that apply to alcholic beverages, antitrust, campaign finance, civil rights, copyright protection, environmental protection, foreign corrupt practices, securities and taxes. While the Company does not expect associates to be experts in legal matters, it holds each associate responsible for being familiar with the laws governing his or her areas of responsibility. Associates should seek advice from the Law Department whenever they have a question concerning the application of the law. From time to time, the Law Department will prepare a "Business Conduct Guide" and circulate it to the appropriate management associates.

Treat all associates fairly, with dignity and with respect. All associates are entitled to a work environment without verbal, physical and sexual harassment. The Company is committed to the principles and procedures described in its Guarantee of Fair Treatment. The Company is also committed to providing equal

---

opportunities for minorities, women, veterans and persons with disabilities. The Company believes promotion of work force diversity is an important objective in its own right, a source of competitive advantage and a requirement of Equal Employment Opportunity laws.

Report financial condition and results of operations fairly and honestly. The Company will keep its books and records according to generally accepted accounting principles and with established finance and accounting policies. Accrual and reserve entries and the capitalization of costs will be used only for legitimate business purposes. All associates will cooperate fully with internal and outside auditors during examinations of the Company's books, records and operations.

Deal honestly and fairly with clients, customers, suppliers and financial partners. The long-term success of the Company depends upon establishing mutually beneficial relationships. While the law requires that we obey the letter of all written contracts and agreements, we will also try to uphold the spirit of all business arrangements.

Avoid conflicts of interest. Associates should avoid actual or potential conflict of interest situations. Consequently, an associate having any interest, direct or indirect (other than an interest of 5% or less in a publicly held company), in any supplier, customer, competitor or franchise of the Company should make prompt disclosure to the Company and obtain approval from the appropriate authority to continue the relationship. Management associates should not offer their skills or services to competitors or engage in outside businesses that compete with or sell goods or services to the Company. Employing immediate family members in direct supervisory/subordinate relationships should be avoided.

Avoid improper giving and receiving of gifts. Exchanging gifts with customers and suppliers is a normal and acceptable business practice. However, giving or receiving gifts of significant value could compromise the objectivity of an associate as well as create the appearance of an improper act. Therefore, gifts that an associate gives or receives in excess of $50 (retail value) must be disclosed to the associate's supervisor and on the annual CP-1 Questionnaire. The supervisor will determine whether the gift should be accepted, turned over to the Company or returned. Gifts of perishable items (e.g., flowers and fruit baskets) or commemorative items (e.g., plaques and framed photographs) are not subject to this $50 limit. They should, however, have little or no intrinsic or resale value. Business entertainment should be lawful, appropriate and within acceptable boundaries of good taste and business purpose.

Safeguard the Company's assets. Personal use of supplies, equipment or premises belonging to the Company or its clients is prohibited, unless a supervisor gives prior permission and arranges adequate compensation. Every associate is responsible for safeguarding Company assets under the associate's control.

Separate personal political activities from the Company's business. The Company encourages each associate's individual participation in the political process. This includes service on governmental bodies and participation in partisan political activities. However, such activities should not interfere with the associate's job responsibilities. Associates should not make political contributions using Company funds or take public positions on behalf of the Company without first obtaining approval from the Company's General Counsel. The Company engages in political activity through the Marriott Political Action Committee (MARPAC). Management associates are encouraged to contribute to MARPAC but should not be forced, intimidated, rewarded or pressured to do so.

Report observed violations of standards. The integrity of the organization is diminished whenever standards are violated. The Company expects associates to report known violations to their supervisors.

Associates can report ethical violations to the Law Department or Internal Audit at any time. The Company will honor all requests for confidentiality. Every business unit and administrative department will establish procedures for associates to report ethical violations on a confidential basis.

Internal Audit will obtain annual certifications (CP-1 Questionnaire) from a broad range of management associates.

Commentary

Marriott's ethical policy makes a strong statement about the firm's ethical guidelines. The nine sections are placed as directives to employees, and leave little room for misinterpretation. The one on gift giving and receiving is especially well done. They are part of the company's booklet, A Manager's Roadmap to Business Success, which contains extensive (almost 30 pages in length) discussion of a range of ethical and policy issues including purchasing, sexual harassment, EEOC issues, and substance abuse among others. This document appears near the end of the booklet, and each employee is asked to sign that they have read and understand these policies.

Mary Kay, Inc.

The Principles We Live By:

° Integrity and the Golden Rule must guide every business decision.

° Quality in our products and services must be a priority in order to deliver value and satisfaction to our customers.

° Praise motivates everyone to reach their full potential.

° Teamwork allows each person to be valued and appreciated by others while contributing to the Company's success.

° Enthusiasm encourages a positive attitude and provides inspiration as we work together to achieve our goals.

° Service should be prompt and proactive to provide convenience with a personal touch.

° Leadership among our sales force and employees must be encouraged and recognized in order to achieve long-term success.

° Balancing our lives, with God, family and career will lead to happy, fulfilled lives.

Commentary

This statement of Mary Kay outlines eight central principles the organization "lives by." It appears significant that integrity is the first one listed. The enthusiasm, praise, leadership and teamwork principles were evident several years ago when Mary Kay Ash gave a presentation that this writer witnessed. Her enthusiasm and subsequent response from the beauty consultants were certainly uplifting. Finally, the "Balancing" principle stresses the importance that the company places on its employees and salespeople leading balanced lives.

Merrill Lynch

Client Focus

Our clients are the driving force behind what we do.
Our company's founder, Charles E. Merrill, declared that the client's interests must come first. Today, client focus is just as imperative as it was in Mr. Merrill's day. In our increasingly competitive industry, success rests not on our ability to sell a certain product or service, but on the degree to which clients value Merrill Lynch as their trusted adviser.

To achieve this stature, it will not be enough merely to meet our clients' expectations. We must constantly strive to exceed them.

Respect for the Individual

We respect dignity of each individual, whether an employee, shareholder, client or member of the general public.
We strive to be a lean, decisive and aggressive organization, but on a personal level to treat each individual with dignity, consideration and respect. This means sharing the credit when credit is due, avoiding public criticism of one another, and encouraging an atmosphere in which openness, cooperation and mutual consultation are the norms. It means following the Golden Rule.

As a company, we will seek, nurture and reward the highest-caliber employees, regardless of race, national origin, religion, gender, age or physical ability. We will encourage this diversity amongst ourselves, realizing it to be an important competitive advantage in the rapidly emerging global marketplace.

Teamwork

**We strive for seamless integration of services. In our clients'
eyes, there is only one Merrill Lynch.**
It is great teams that win, not loose affiliations of all-stars.
Therefore, we expect real teamwork throughout our company,
and we reward people for it. We are committed to an honest
sharing of both risks and rewards with one another, so that when
clients achieve their goals, everyone at Merrill Lynch benefits.

Our people and resources are unmatched in our industry, yet
they are not enough to guarantee continued success. In order to
be our clients' trusted adviser, we must take pride in working as
a team — at all levels and across all boundaries — bringing all of
the diverse skills and resources of Merrill Lynch to bear in
solving client problems.

Responsible Citizenship

**As the company that brought Wall Street to Main Street and
the world, we seek to improve the quality of life in the
communities where our employees live and work.**
Responsible citizenship means that we are committed to giving
something back to the communities in which we earn our
livelihood. We encourage employee volunteerism and
community involvement. Both as a corporation and as
individuals, we support education, the cultural arts, the
environment and community services in the U.S. and around the
world.

And, we advocate public policies — such as open global markets
and enhanced incentives for savings and investment — that
promote long-term economic growth and opportunity around
the world.

Integrity

No one's personal bottom line is more important than the reputation of our firm.

Our most important corporate asset is the great Merrill Lynch "tradition of trust" — our company's long-standing reputation for integrity in the marketplace.

As beneficiaries of this great tradition, we will be tolerant of ordinary mistakes made in the course of business; we will not tolerate lapses in ethics or integrity.

While "R.O.I." does not appear in our financial statements, Merrill Lynch enjoys a return on integrity that we will protect, whatever the cost, as the bedrock of our prosperity and our pride.

Commentary

These five values guide the operations of Merrill Lynch and are used in the evaluation of employees. The fact that customers are the most important stakeholder seems clear. The principles of respect for the individual, teamwork, integrity (including trust) and responsible citizenship signal the importance of an ethical basis for the company. The new CEO indicated in a speech at Notre Dame that these values are "not negotiable" and possibly the number one challenge internationally is to live them. He used the analogy of a road and stated that these principles lay out a "highway of acceptable behavior." In the international arena, he stated that the road may be narrow and winding, but the company always wants to be on the road of accepted practice.

Metal Leve

Ethical Commitment

- Be conscious that the company does not constitute an end in itself, but that it is also an instrument to social development.
- Develop a personal technological effort, through which it seeks to follow the external technological progress.
- Seek more capital than loans.
- Be concerned about the consumer, fulfilling his or her needs in what relates to quality and price.
- Be conscious of the need for an adequate relationship with the workers, recognizing their fundamental importance, trying to anticipate their fair claims and examining the ones submitted to the company with objectivity.
- Maintain independence toward the government, following the law strictly.
- Strengthen labor unions and business associations, establishing with the latter a permanent relationship of constructive cooperation.
- Know how to coexist with the foreign firm, recognizing the contribution it has given and can still give to our country and do not hesitate, for a mere prejudice, to associate itself to external investment, whenever the circumstances advise so, even though trying, as a rule, to maintain control of its enterprise.
- Support cultural and educational activities, considering this a social duty.
- Intensify the professional administration and also intensify the relationship with the university, aiming the formation of qualified professionals still insufficient in number, to cope with the technological revolution through which we have gone.
- And above all, be free to make managerial decisions, free from the government's tutorship; do not seek the technobureaucracy's consent at every step, since even with the best intention, it does not have the omniscient gift, and

cannot know better than the business person what is best for the company.

—Dr. Jose E. Mindlin, President

Comment

The ethical commitment statement was developed for this Brazilian firm by its former CEO. It addresses issues dealing with the government and labor unions that are not prevalent in the United States today. The first statement deals with the larger social role of the firm, and the sixth states that following the law is a must. The final one seeks independence between business and government. While this statement takes a more social vs. moral perspective than most of the others contained in the book, it does represent an attempt to codify the principles that one executive believed his company should follow.

The Nahser Agency

O̲ur purpose is to create and implement outstanding ideas to help our clients' businesses grow, benefit the user, and contribute to the well-being of society.

T̲o provide this vital service, our experience has led us to this strategy: *Creating enduring relationships by going beyond expectations.*

W̲e do this by living certain deeply held, shared values:

Personal Values	Organizational Values
ATTITUDE	GROWTH
INTEGRITY	FAIRNESS
HARD WORK	RESPONSIBILITY
TALENT	RESPECT

Our people:
Are passionate about advertising,
Work effectively in groups.
"Gladly learn and gladly teach."*
Wish to be recognized and fairly
compensated for outstanding work.
November 21, 1980. (Updated November 20, 1992)

* *Chaucer*

Commentary

This short statement affirms the three roles that an advertising agency should play in the first sentence. Both organizational and personal values are explicitly stated. Although the lists are different, the central role that basic ethical precepts in guiding individual employees as well as corporate behavior are clear. The CEO, Ron Nahser, has articulated his philosophies on "community" as a guiding principle in the firm (1997); Nahser's personal values and this statement were featured in a recent book (Liebeg 1994, 149–52). His application of these values is also evident in a case study examining an ad campaign for the toy industry (Laczniak and Murphy 1993, 146–47).

Nalco Chemical Company

Equal Employment Opportunity Policy

Nalco Chemical Company is committed to providing equal employment opportunities.

Our policy promises equal opportunity for every individual in every phase of our employment relationship. This is a program with far-reaching implications. This objective cannot be achieved just by repeating the words from time to time. We intend to live up to our commitment through a combination of understanding and action on the part of each employee.

Nalco believes that employees welcome the challenge which comes with being expected to perform to the best of their abilities. Nalco expects good performance, rewards employees on the basis of performance, and intends to provide each individual an equal opportunity to perform.

There are four essential reasons why it is important to commit the time and effort necessary to accomplish the goal of equal employment opportunity:

FIRST
It's the right thing to do. Everyone should be treated with equal consideration and offered equal opportunity. The measure of employees lies in how they perform their jobs, not in their race, sex, age, color, national origin, religion, veteran status, or physical or mental disability.

SECOND
It utilizes valuable human abilities. Waste of human talent occurs when individuals or groups of persons are denied good jobs, promotions, and opportunities to develop their potential.

THIRD
It provides an atmosphere of fairness. Nalco, and consequently all of us who are employed by Nalco, stand to benefit materially from having and living up to a reputation of fairness. We will succeed if people recognize us as a company that practices equal opportunity with our employees, customers, suppliers, and the public.

FOURTH

In addition, it's the law. The Equal Pay Act of 1963, Title VII of the 1964 Civil Rights Act and Executive Order 11246 (race, color, religion, sex, sexual harassment, and national origin), Age Discrimination in Employment Act of 1967, Section 503 of the Rehabilitation Act of 1973 (disabled), and the Vietnam Era Veterans Readjustment Assistance Act of 1974, and the Americans with Disabilities Act of 1990, the Civil Rights Act of 1991 and relevant amendments, require that Nalco practice equal employment opportunity.

Affirmative Action Programs

In order to be as effective as possible in carrying out our commitment to equal employment opportunity, we have implemented Affirmative Action Programs in each Division, Department and Group within Nalco. These programs have one general objective: to make sure that everyone gets an equal opportunity in every phase of employment—that no one, or no group, is unlawfully discriminated against. To achieve this objective, we have re-emphasized and broadened our efforts in the following areas:

RECRUITMENT

We will make every effort to recruit more effectively, contacting specialized schools and colleges and community organizations concerned with the placement of women, racial minorities, veterans and person with disabilities.

REFERRAL

We will make ever effort to encourage all employees, including women, racial minorities, veterans and persons with disabilities to refer to us their friends and acquaintances who are seeking employment.

HIRING

We will make every effort to hire women, racial minorities, veterans and disabled persons and those over 40 years of age into positions where it is evident that such representation does not constitute external workforce participation availability.

Further, we will continuously review all job descriptions to eliminate non-job related requirements.

TRAINING
We administer programs to train employees for jobs and to assist supervisors and managers in improving their employee relations skills. We make every effort to provide employees the opportunity to participate in training that will enable them to develop potential abilities and prepare for promotion.

PROMOTION
We periodically review the procedures by which we select people for promotion to assure that they are administered fairly to all employees. We pay special attention to opportunities in higher job classications for women, racial minorities, veterans, and disabled employees. Where it appears that there are inequities, we make available special training and development programs to prepare people for promotion into better jobs. Our goal is equal opportunity at all job levels.

OTHER EMPLOYMENT PRACTICES
It is Nalco's practice to continuously review and correct any inequities in its policies of compensation, benefits, discipline and termination.

Communicating Our Program
While our policy of equal opportunity must apply, first of all, to employees, it has broader applications. It is equally important that we treat other people fairly—those who buy from us, perform contract work for us or supply goods and services to us. Following are some examples of action programs we have developed to carry out this commitment:

DISSEMINATING OUR POLICY
Our policy on equal employment opportunity continues to be made known both inside and outside of Nalco. Internally, we communicate our policy through media such as new employee orientation sessions, meetings, training programs, employee publications, films and posters. Externally, we publicize our policy through employment agencies, community and

professional organizations, advertising media and other appropriate means.

ADVERTISING

Our policy of non-discrimination is also reflected in advertising done by Nalco. We are committed to including women, racial minorities, those over 40 years of age and persons with disabilities in our advertisements as a way of indicating publicly that we accept, serve and employ everyone equally. We are also committed to the use of minority-owned and oriented media such as newspapers and magazines for appropriate advertising messages.

COOPERATION WITH COMMUNITY ORGANIZATIONS

We cooperate with, and participate in, community organizations concerned with the employment of women, racial minorities, veterans, persons with disabilities and those protected by age discrimination laws.

CONTRACTORS AND SUPPLIERS

We are continuing our efforts to find and develop new sources for the materials and services we buy, including enterprises owned by women and racial minorities.

Implementing Our Program

The responsibility for making our equal opportunity policies and programs work rests with each Nalco employee. Because we have many employees and many locations, certain people have been given the responsibility for implementing the programs.

1. The appropriate Vice President or President of each Division, Department or Group is responsible for approving and implementing its Affirmative Action Program. The EEO department maintains records of applicant flow, new hires, transfers, promotions and terminations, for auditing and generating reports on progress being made toward Affirmative Action Program goals.

2. The Manager, EEO as the principal consultant on equal employment opportunity affairs for Nalco, provides assistance to all managers in meeting goals of the Affirmative Action Programs, is the liaison between Nalco and government agencies

assigned to monitor our EEO activities, audits practices within each Division, Department or Group to assure that company policies are being carried out, and reports to corporate management on EEO developments both inside and outside of Nalco.

3. All managers and supervisors work to make equal employment opportunity a continuing reality at Nalco. In order to carry out the policies of equal employment opportunity, managers and supervisors will do the following:

a. Review all position descriptions and job specifications objectively to assure hiring practices which provide equal employment opportunity to all qualified candidates.

b. Provide equal consideration for qualified women, racial minorities, veterans, persons with diabilities, and those protected by laws concerning age, national origin and religion when hiring or promoting to assignments requiring greater skill, effort, or responsibility.

c. Provide equal consideration for all employees under Nalco's compensation program.

d. Maintain an awareness of problems specifically related to the employment and advancement of people protected by laws concerning sex (including sexual harassment), race, national origin, religion, physical and mental disabilities, age, and veteran status, taking constructive measures to remedy them.

e. Communicate Nalco's equal employment opportunity policies to all subordinates, to achieve compliance at every level.

Nalco's success in providing equal employment opportunity is dependent on the action and attitude of each Nalco manager and supervisor. The effectiveness of their contributions to Affirmative Action Programs will be considered in evaluating their total job performance.

Commentary

Nalco's statement on equal opportunity and affirmative action is one of the most complete of any firm. Not only does it spell out the principles that guide the firm, but also the implementation of the program is clearly articulated. While some firms are placing less stress on this topic or are only providing vague general statements about it, Nalco has made its views widely known. By using words like dissemination, communication, promotion and advertising, the company signals how seriously they take the objective of a more diverse workforce.

Nortel

NORTEL'S CORE VALUES

We create superior value for our customers.

We work to provide shareholder value.

Our people are our strength.

We share one vision. We are one team.

We have only one standard—excellence.

We embrace change and reward innovation.

We fulfill our commitments and act with integrity.

"As an operating principle, we will conduct our business honestly and ethically wherever we operate in the world. Acting with integrity builds credibility—that fragile, intangible asset that's so hard to gain, so easy to lose, and so difficult to regain. Ethical conduct is the way we protect our credibility as a company, establish respect for the dignity of every individual, earn the trust of our partners and customers, and define the character of our business."

Jean C. Monty, President and Chief Executive Officer

At Northern Telecom (Nortel), we recognize the importance of credibility, integrity and trustworthiness to our success as a business. We are committed to upholding high ethical standards in all our operations, everywhere in the world. We believe in the principles of honesty, fairness, and respect for individual and community freedoms.

Living up to both the letter and the spirit of this commitment is not always an easy task. As a large and diverse corporation working globally, we recognize that while there is some level of agreement the world over on what constitutes honest and ethical business practice, there can also be valid differences of opinion.

In our working lives, we often experience situations where the "right thing to do" is not immediately apparent. Loyalties—to our fellow employees, to managers, customers and suppliers, to our families, our communities, the environment, the corporation as a whole, and to ourselves—may seem to conflict. When we're faced with a complicated situation, it can be difficult to decide where the ethical path lies.

The standards and expectations outlined in Nortel's *Code of Business Conduct* are intended as a guide to making the right choice. They are included on our website: www.nortel.com/cool/ethics/

Core Values:
A Guide to Ethical Business Practice

New ways of organizing people and work within the corporation are giving each of us more decision-making responsibility. Given the complexity and constantly changing nature of our work and our world, no book of hard-and-fast rules-however long and detailed-could ever adequately cover all the dilemmas people face. In this context, every Nortel employee is asked to take leadership in ethical decision making.

Person Values and Corporate Integrity

In most situations, our personal values and honesty will guide us to the right decision. But in our capacity as employees and representatives of Nortel, we must also always consider how our actions affect the integrity and credibility of the corporation as a whole. Our business ethics must reflect the standard of conduct outlined in this document—a standard grounded in the corporation's values, and governing Nortel's relationships with all stakeholders.

Our decisions as to what is ethical business practice in a Nortel context must be guided by the seven Core Values that form the fundamental basis of our conduct as a business. From these statements stem a series of commitments that we as Nortel employees make to each other, to shareholders, customers, suppliers, and the communities in which we do business.

A Shared Responsibility

The final core value emphasizes our intention to fulfill our commitments and to do so with integrity. Integrity means "wholeness"—it means that all the parts are aligned and work together. It means, for example, that each individual within the corporation is doing his or her best to live by the standard of business conduct outlined in the *Code*.

"Acting with integrity" also means that while we may not always be sure of every answer, we will not say one thing and then do another. We will not make promises that we have no intention of keeping or cannot be reasonably sure we will be able to keep. We will strive to the best of our ability to support all the commitments that the corporation has made to conducting business in an honest and ethical manner.

Commentary

The core values and material reprinted above come from the first few pages of Nortel's Code of Business Conduct entitled "Acting with Integrity." Much more detailed information is contained in the full (twenty-five page) document. In a separate memo accompanying the code book, CEO Monty indicated that this '96 revision "commits us to a higher standard of practice than we may have followed in the past," "has been shaped by the input of more than 1,000 employees," and "illustrates how Nortel's Core Values translate into ethical business practices." The focus is on conducting business according to time honored principles. However, the paragraphs following the quote indicate that the global, complex world often makes ethical decisions difficult to achieve. Recognition of the interplay between personal and corporate values is articulated nicely and the last section above spells out what the final core value regarding integrity at Nortel means.

J. C. Penney

The Penney Idea

To serve the public, as nearly as we can, to its complete satisfaction.

To expect for the service we render a fair remuneration and not all the profit the traffice will bear.

To do all in our power to pack the customer's dollar full of value, quality and satisfaction.

To continue to train ourselves and our associates so that the service we give will be more and more intelligently performed.

To improve constantly the human factor in our business.

To reward men and women in our organization through participation in what the business produces.

To test our every policy, method and act in this wise: "Does it square with what is right and just?"

Commentary

This corporate credo originated in 1913. The statement's English is a bit dated, but the message is as clear today as it was then. Commitment to customer service (a 1990s phenomenon) and fair treatment of employees represent timeless values that Penney identified long ago. One little known fact is that J. C. Penney's initial choice for the name of his chain was the Golden Rule Stores. He believed strongly that the application and adherence to this concept should pervade his company's decisions. The Penney Idea is widely cited by employees as serving as a guidepost for company operations and individual actions (Oliverio 1989).

Procter & Gamble

Purpose

WE WILL PROVIDE PRODUCTS OF SUPERIOR
QUALITY AND VALUE THAT IMPROVE THE
LIVES OF THE WORLD'S CUSTOMERS.

AS A RESULT, CONSUMERS WILL REWARD US
WITH LEADERSHIP SALES AND PROFIT
GROWTH, ALLOWING OUR PEOPLE, OUR
SHAREHOLDERS AND THE COMMUNITIES IN
WHICH WE LIVE AND WORK TO PROSPER.

Core Values

P&G PEOPLE We attract and recruit the finest people
in the world. We build our organization from within, promoting
and rewarding people without regard to any difference
unrelated to performance. We act on the conviction that the men
and women of Procter & Gamble will always be our most
important asset.

LEADERSHIP We are all leaders in our area of
responsibility, with a deep commitment to deliver leadership
results. We have a clear vision of where we are going. We focus
our resources to achieve leadership objectives and strategies. We
develop the capability to deliver our strategies and eliminate
organizational barriers.

OWNERSHIP We accept personal accountability to

meet the business needs, improve our systems and help others improve their effectiveness. We all act like owners, treating the Company's assets as our own and behaving with the Company's long-term success in mind.

INTEGRITY We always try to do the right thing. We are honest and straightforward with each other. We operate within the letter and spirit of the law. We uphold the values and principles of P&G in every action and decision. We are data-based and intellectually honest in advocating proposals, including recognizing risks.

PASSION FOR WINNING We are determined to be the best at doing what matters most. We have a healthy dissatisfaction with the status quo. We have a compelling desire to improve and to win in the marketplace.

TRUST We respect our P&G colleagues, customers, consumers and treat them as we want to be treated. We have confidence in each other's capabilities and intentions. We believe that people work best when there is a foundation of trust.

Commentary

These two documents outline P&G's overall philosophy and values. The strong emphasis on "people" in both (improving the lives of the world's consumers and employees as the most important asset) reflects the importance of the human dimension of the firm's activities. Inclusion of both integrity and trust in the core values is a sign that ethical principles are very important. The company reinforces these short statements with two longer booklets—"Worldwide Business Conduct Manual" and "Your Personal Responsibility." In a recent speech the current CEO, John Pepper (1997), articulated his view on this topic: "I can't overemphasize the importance of maintaining a rigidly ethical behavior. There can be short-term costs, to be sure—a lost sale, lost market share, even public perception issues—but the longer term consequence of not behaving ethically is far, far greater."

Progressive Corporation

Core Values:

Progressive has its values. We want them to be understood and embraced by all Progressive people. They dictate our decision and actions. They cause us to be different and to succeed.

Integrity. We revere truth and practice open disclosure. We adhere to high ethical standards, report completely, encourage disclosing bad news and welcome disagreement.

Golden Rule. We respect all people. We deal with people as we would like them to deal with us. Shareholders, employees, customers and suppliers are partners.

Objectives. We carefully document, continually review and clearly communicate Progressive's values, mission, and strategies. Individual objectives are negotiated, documented and are the basis for performance evaluation.

Excellence. For Progressive, excellence means doing better than we did before. We seek motivated, intelligent, educated people who understand and embrace our values, work hard, have fun working, are flexible and often creative. Compensation is based on results and promotion on results and ability.

Profit. We seek both superior long-term profit and growth to provide outstanding shareholder returns and exciting opportunities for our people. We invest in new business as long as we expect superior profit and growth. Profit is more important than growth. If we cannot obtain adequate prices for competitive, regulatory and other reasons, we will not write that insurance or sell that service.

Commentary

Progressive's values statement is unique in several ways. First, integrity is defined as encompassing not only ethical principles but also coming forward with negative information. Second, this document is the only one reprinted here that includes the Golden Rule as a value. Third, excellence is defined in terms of employees more than products. Finally, objectives and profits are discussed in philosophical terms, not just as business ones.

Protective Life Corporation

Protective Life's Mission and Values

Protective Life Corporation provides financial security through life and health insurance and investment products. Our vision is to enhance the quality of life of our customers, our stockholders, and our people.

We hold to three preeminent values—quality, serving people, and growth—which by tradition and choice transcend all others. They are the foundation of our aspirations, our plans, our best energies, and our life together in this Company.

Quality

The heart of quality is integrity. Quality is the cornerstone on which all our activity rests—quality products, services, people, and investments. We strive for superior quality and continuous quality improvement in everything we do.

Serving People

Serving people is vital. We find our ultimate reward in the service and support of three groups:

Customers: Our customers come first. We prosper only to the extent that we create long-term relationships with satisfied customers. We do so in discerning their needs and responding to them; in providing high value, distinctive products; in prudent investment of policyholder funds; in systems, information, and counsel which help our customers solve problems; and in prompt, accurate, innovative, and courteous service which is the best in the business.

Stockholders: Our stockholders provide the equity essential for our success. We are stewards of their investment and must return a profit to them. Profit is essential for implementing our commitment to quality, serving people, and growth. It is a critical measurement of our performance. Our objective is to rank at the top of the industry in long-range earnings growth and return on equity.

Protective People: The accomplishment of our mission depends on all Protective people working together. We want our

---

people to enjoy their work and take pride in Protective Life, its mission and values. We are committed to opportunity and training for all to help us fulfill our potential; open, candid communication; the input, initiative, and empowerment of all our people; the encouragement of one another; and creating a place where a zeal to serve our customers, stockholders, and each other permeates the Company.

Growth

We are dedicated to long-term growth in sales, revenues, and profit, not only for our stockholders but also for personal growth and development of Protective people. We achieve growth through resourceful marketing, superior service, and acquisitions. Growth is critical for improving quality and serving people. It is essential to maintaining a position of strength in our marketplace and attracting and retaining high caliber people.

Commentary

This one statement combines Protective's mission, vision and values. Quality of life and service are themes running through the entire document. Although it is not explained, the first sentence in Quality stating that the "heart of quality is integrity" affirms the ethical posture of the company. People are very important to the firm and the primacy of customers is clearly articulated. The section on employees gives the sense that the company is strongly committed to their welfare.

Quad/Graphics

Trust in Trust at Quad/Graphics

- The Trust of Teamwork. Employees trust that together they will do better than as individuals apart.

- The Trust of Responsibility. Employees trust that each will carry his/her fair share of the load.

- The Trust of Productivity. Customers trust that work will be produced to the most competitive levels of pricing, quality and innovation.

- The Trust of Management. Shareholders, customers and employees trust that the company will make decisive judgments for the long-term rather than the short-term goals or today's profit.

- The Trust of Think-Small. We all trust in each other; we regard each other as persons of equal rank; we respect the dignity of the individual by recognizing not only the individual accomplishments, but the feelings and needs of the individual and family as well; and we all share the same goals and purposes in life.

Commentary

Trust is obviously the theme for the Quad/Graphics' ethics statement. Employees are the focus of the first two types of trust, customers for the third and all stakeholders should trust in management. The egalitarian philosophy of the firm is spelled out in the "think-small" type of trust, and the final clause presents a consistent purpose to which employees hopefully aspire. The word trust is sometimes viewed as superior to the term ethics, and this company has done an excellent job of accentuating the importance of trust in a business setting.

Reell Precision Manufacturing

Our RPM Direction

RPM is a team dedicated to the purpose of operating a business based on the practical application of Judeo-Christian values for the mutual benefit of co-workers and their families, customers, shareholders, suppliers, and community. We are committed to provide an environment where there is no conflict between work and moral/ethical values or family responsibilities and where everyone is treated justly.

The tradition of excellence at RPM has grown out of a commitment to excellence rooted in the character of our Creator. Instead of driving each other towards excellence, we strive to free each other to grow and express the desire for excellence that is within all of us. By adhering to the following principles, we are challenged to work and make decisions consistent with God's purpose for creation according to our individual understanding.

DO WHAT IS RIGHT We are committed to do what is right even when it does not seem to be profitable, expedient, or conventional.

DO OUR BEST In our understanding of excellence we embrace a commitment to continuous improvement in everything we do. It is our commitment to encourage, teach, equip, and free each other to do and become all that we were intended to be.

TREAT OTHERS AS WE WOULD LIKE TO BE TREATED

SEEK INSPIRATIONAL WISDOM by looking outside ourselves, especially with respect to decisions having far-reaching and unpredictable consequences, but we will act only when the action is confirmed unanimously by others concerned.

We currently manufacture motion control devices for a world market. Our goal is to continually improve our ability to meet customer needs. How we accomplish our mission is important to us. The following groups are fundamental to our success:

CO-WORKERS People are the heart of RPM. We are committed to providing a secure opportunity to earn a livelihood and pursue personal growth.

CUSTOMERS Customers are the lifeblood of RPM. Our products and services must be the best in meeting and exceeding customer expectations.

SHAREHOLDERS We recognize that profitability is necessary to continue in business, reach full potential, and fulfill our responsibilities to shareholders. We expect profits, but our commitments to co-workers and customers come before short-term profits.

SUPPLIERS We treat our suppliers as valuable partners in all our activities.

COMMUNITY We will use a share of our energy and resources to meet the needs of our local and global community.

We find that in following these principles we can experience enjoyment, happiness and peace of mind in our work and in our individual lives.

Commentary

The RPM statement is distinctive in its focus on Judeo-Christian values and use of God in it. The definition of excellence used by this company is different from others reprinted in this volume. The four principles offer inspirational personal and professional advice (i.e., the Golden Rule is the third point). Five stakeholder groups are identified and the priority of importance is clearly stated in the one dealing with shareholders. The final sentence in the document gives one the impression that RPM is an satisfying place to work with a strong commitment to spiritual values.

Rhone-Poulenc Rorer, Inc.

Being the Best Means:

◻ Being the BEST at satisfying the needs of everyone we serve: patients, healthcare professionals, employees, communities, governments and shareholders;

◻ Being BETTER AND FASTER than our competitors at discovering and bringing to market important new medicines in selected therapeutic areas;

◻ Operating with the HIGHEST professional and ethical standards in all our activities, building on the Rhone-Poulenc and Rorer heritage of integrity;

◻ Being seen as the BEST place to work, attracting and retaining talented people at all levels by creating an environment that encourages them to develop their potential to the fullest;

◻ Generating consistently BETTER results than our competitors, through innovation and a total commitment to quality in everything we do.

Commentary

This statement is very aspirational in tone. In fact, it appears to use Maslow's highest level of needs—self-actualization—as its ideal. It is more competitive in tone than many of the other statements contained in this volume with the second and fifth ones dealing directly with competitors. The third and fourth statements, though, are ones with strong ethical overtones. Rhone-Poulenc Rorer's motivating principles of "being all you can be" are clear to the reader.

Rich Products Corporation

Our Strategy

We will achieve our World Class Mission by working together as a team in a total quality effort to:

◻ **Impress Our Customers**

Provide exceptional services to our external and internal customers the first time and every time.

◻ **Improve, Improve, Improve!**

Continuously improve the quality and value of the goods we produce and services we provide.

◻ **Empower People**

Unleash the talents of all our associates by creating an environment that is safe, that recognizes and rewards their achievements, and encourages their participation and growth.

◻ **Work Smarter**

Drive out all waste of time effort and material—all the barriers and extra steps that keep us from doing our jobs right.

◻ **Do The Right Thing!**

Maintain the highest standards of integrity and ethical conduct and behave as a good citizen in our communities.

Commentary

This short statement is very uplifting. The active tense of the five boldface headings both implore and guide employees. The firm appears to be very committed to quality and continual improvement. The final statement leaves the reader with the feeling that Rich Products is very serious about rewarding ethical and responsible actions both inside and outside the company.

St. Luke's

Total Role in Society (TRS)

Ten Principles of TRS

1. It is the potential of all business to benefit society. The maximization of that benefit will be a company's primary marketing differentiation in the 21st century.

2. In the future, a company will have to be a trusted social citizen before it can sell or advertise effectively.

3. In the next century, the essential selling point of a company will be its Total Role in Society. TRS is an evaluation of an organization among the totality of its stakeholders.

4. TRS reflects the principle that the maximization of profits is the *requirement* of business, but not its purpose.

5. The persuasiveness of any message relies upon the quality of its reception among all of its stakeholders: shareholders, employees, clients, vendors, customers, competitors, the local community, the environment, families of employees, consumer groups, the legislature.

6. Companies that are seen and believed to be delivering positive contributions to those they touch will be rewarded economically and encouraged to continue.

7. A company can better maximize its profits if it sells or advertises its products or services as part of an integrated TRS strategy that holistically and honestly embraces all of its constituents.

8. There is a law of reciprocity between communicator and recipient. The recipient must be rewarded, not just spoken to, with qualities integral to the communication itself.

9. The greatest barrier to a corporation's success is a misalignment of intent and behavior.

10. Communications are a magnifier. Advertising and public relations no longer control perceptions; they are lenses that magnify alignment as well as misalignment.

Four Steps to Achieving TRS

1. Qualitative audit of a company's mission, operations, products, services, and communications: Who are your stakeholders and what do they need? What is your company's perceived company reputation? What is your company's *ideal* company reputation?

2. Strategic evaluation: What can your company deliver from its core competency to society that will enhance your company's reputation and maximize its value? ("I'm IBM and I'll make the planet smarter.") What current activities are in line with this TRS? ("I'm Delta and I banned smoking on all worldwide flights.") What current activities are not in line with this TRS? ("I'm Reebok and kids kill each other for my shoes.")

3. Design: Creative development of communications, programs, and policies that aggressively enrich a company's relationship with all of its stakeholders.

4. Implementation: Instead of merely communicating your values within the organization, how can you actually enroll everyone in its ideation? (Self-generated persuasion.)

Commentary

This UK-based advertising agency uses ethics as a key differentiating feature. St. Luke's was created with a communal ownership structure, called QUEST *(Qualifying Employee Shareholder Trust). Its ten principles outline how the company hopes to accomplish its business and social mission. The Total Role in Society is a four-step stakeholder oriented process. TRS was originally formulated when the agency managers were employees of Chiat/Day. An article examining the unique posture of St. Luke's states "they evangelize the power of ethics in business" (Alburty 1997).*

Saturn

VALUES

We, at SATURN, are committed to being one of the world's most successful car companies by adhering to the following values:

COMMITMENT TO CUSTOMER ENTHUSIASM
We continually exceed the expectations of internal and external customers for products and services that are world leaders in cost, quality, and customer satisfaction. Our customers know that we really care about them.

COMMITMENT TO EXCEL
There is no place for mediocrity and half-hearted efforts at SATURN. We accept responsibility, accountability and authority for overcoming obstacles and reaching beyond the best. We choose to excel in every aspect of our business, including return on investment.

TEAMWORK
We are dedicated to singleness of purpose through the effective involvement of members, suppliers, dealers, neighbors and all other stakeholders. A fundamental tenet of our philosophy is the belief that effective teams engage the talents of individual members while encouraging team growth.

TRUST AND RESPECT FOR THE INDIVIDUAL
We have nothing of greater value than our people! We believe that demonstrating respect for the uniqueness of every individual builds a team of confident, creative members possessing a high degree of initiative, self-respect, and self-discipline.

CONTINUOUS IMPROVEMENT
We know that sustained success depends on our ability to continually improve the quality, cost and timeliness of our products and services. We are providing opportunity for personal, professional, and organizational growth and innovation for all SATURN stakeholders.

PHILOSOPHY

We, the Saturn Team, in concert with the UAW and General Motors, believe that meeting the needs of Customers, Saturn Members, Suppliers, Dealers and Neighbors is fundamental to fulfilling our mission.

To meet our customers' needs:

¤   Our products and services must be world leaders in value and satisfaction.

To meet our members' needs:

¤   We will create a sense of belonging in an environment of mutual trust, respect and dignity.

¤   We believe that all people want to be involved in decisions that affect them, care about their jobs and each other, take pride in themselves and in their contributions and want to share in the success of their efforts.

¤   We will develop the tools, training and education for each member, recognizing individual skills and knowledge.

¤   We believe that creative, motivated, responsible team members who understand that change is critical to success are Saturn's most important asset.

To meet our suppliers' and dealers' needs:

¤   We will strive to create real partnerships with them.

¤   We will be open and fair in our dealings, reflecting trust, respect and their importance to Saturn.

¤   We want dealers and suppliers to feel ownership in Saturn's mission and philosophy as their own.

To meet the needs of our neighbors, the communities in which we live and operate:

¤   We will be good citizens, protect the environment and conserve natural resources.

¤   We will seek to cooperate with government at all levels and strive to be sensitive, open and candid in all our public statements.

By continuously operating according to this philosophy, we will fulfill our mission.

© Saturn Corporation, used with permission.

Commentary

Saturn promotes itself as a different type of automobile manufacturer. This values and philosophy statement provides insight into the firm's perspective. The first two values stipulate the "commitments" of Saturn to customer enthusiasm and to excel. These words are chosen carefully and set the company apart from most competitors because virtually all of their buyers are enthusiastic about their cars and the service they receive. The philosophy document uses the term "members" to denote employees. This is more than a word substitution in that teamwork is not only a value, but a way of doing business between management and labor. In fact, these documents which are distributed on laminated cards are the result of interactions between union and management. The other unique word used in the philosophy statement is calling the community stakeholder "neighbors" which personalizes the relationship between the company and the locations where they operate. The phrase "what's the right thing to do?" is used often at Saturn.

Sears

Professional Ethics.............It all starts with doing the right thing for the right reason.

While working as a Sears Associate, you will be faced with making tough decisions that will affect your commitment to fair, honest and responsible actions. In order to assist you, Sears has adopted a Code of Conduct. We'll be discussing several important points covered in the code that relate to you. Naturally, any discussion can neither anticipate nor answer all the questions you may possibly have. So, if you ever find yourself in a situation where you are not sure what the right thing to do is, you have several options, including the following:

- Ask your Supervisor or Unit Manager for help

- Ask your Human Resource representative for a complete copy of the Code of Conduct

- You can consult confidentially with an Ethics Office Assistant at **1-800-8ASSIST** (1-800-827-7478). If you are seeking guidance or straight answers regarding subjects like the Code of Conduct issues, interpretation of company policy, work place harassment or discrimination, selling practices, or concerns about theft, drug abuse or general ethics questions, please call **1-800-8ASSIST**.

The whole business reputation of Sears, Roebuck rests in the hands of its people. Sears is confident all its Associates will continue to be committed to this endeavor.

Now let's see what it means to do the right thing for the right reason:

> **FAIR DEALING:** You are expected to deal fairly, honestly and responsibly with all customers, fellow associates, and anyone else you come in contact with while representing Sears. With regard to customers, this duty requires you to conduct sales in a truthful and accurate manner, always maintaining the highest of ethical standards. With regard to fellow associates and others you may come in contact with, this responsibility requires you to treat them with respect and dignity, and in the same manner that you wish to be

treated. This requires you to act honestly and fairly in all your dealings with Sears.

CONDUCT IN THE WORKPLACE: While employed by Sears, you are expected to conduct yourself in a professional and businesslike manner. Inappropriate work place behavior such as discrimination, harassment, or the use or distribution of alcohol or drugs is never permitted.

CONFLICT OF INTEREST: While employed by Sears, you are expected to act in the best interest of the company, and to avoid activities that may conflict with this obligation. Activities such as working for a competitor, investing in or doing business with companies that do business with Sears, receiving gifts other than benefits from companies that do business with Sears, and employing or supervising relatives or friends can all potentially conflict with your employment at Sears. If you think you may have a conflict of interest, please consult with your immediate Supervisor or Unit Manager.

COMPANY PROPERTY AND RECORDS: You are expected to protect and safeguard Sears property including merchandise, cash, company records, employee services, and confidential information at all times, and to use this responsibility is the obligation to report any misuse of company property, or conduct you believe might threaten the security of this property. You are also expected to create and maintain only truthful and accurate company records. This duty requires that you ring up sales in proper accounts, accurately account for inventory, and truthfully fill out time cards and benefit forms. Additionally, because of the sensitive nature of business records, this responsibility also requires you to maintain their confidentiality both during and after your employment with Sears.

COMPLYING WITH THE LAW: You are expected to strictly adhere to all applicable laws and regulations in effect where the company does business. This duty requires you to avoid engaging in any unfair or deceptive sales practices, including **"BAIT and SWITCH"***, charging customers for goods or services that were not delivered, or approved, and any other unfair sales activities. This duty also requires you to comply with all work place safety, and environmental protection rules and regulations in your unit. Included in this responsibility is the obligation to report any suspected illegal conduct to your supervisor, unit manager or the Office of Ethics and Business Policy.

*ADVERTISED MERCHANDISE (BAIT and SWITCH): At Sears we have always believed in presenting our products in an honest manner. In 1977, we signed a Consent Order with the Federal Trade Commission about the advertising and sale of major home appliances. The requirements of this Order apply to all advertising and sales of merchandise and services offered by Sears. If your job involves advertising or sales, you must read and sign Bulletin M13 which contains the detailed requirements of the Consent Order. At a minimum, Sears policy requires the following:

- When a customer responds to an advertisement, take the customer directly to the advertised item, describe its features and benefits in a positive manner, and offer to sell the item to the customer.

- Never misrepresent our merchandise; for example, by demonstrating or displaying merchandise in a way that makes it appear that there is something wrong with it—or that it is less useful than it really is. Don't make false or misleading comparisons between advertised merchandise or other merchandise in the same line. Also, never misrepresent a competitor's merchandise or services.

- If you run out of advertised merchandise before the end of the sale, you may write up orders or offer rainchecks for customers at the advertised price, and for delivery as soon as more stock is available. Or, it may be decided to offer the customer equal or better quality merchandise at the same price as the advertised item. If the customer wants the advertised item however, write up the order.

MAKING THE RIGHT CALL: The right choice isn't always obvious—seek advice from your manager or call ETHICS ASSIST at 1-800-8ASSIST (1-800-827-7478) for clarification. A good way to judge yourself is by sharing your decision with your supervisor or unit manager.

Commentary

This Sears statement on professional ethics in selling is one of the most explicit by any firm. It outlines three ethical responsibilities (Fair Dealing, Conduct in the Workplace, and Conflict of Interest) and follows with three legal requirements with which sales associates are expected to comply. The discussion of bait and switch gives very clear guidance. By both beginning and ending with the ASSIST line information, the company stresses that there are resources available to support this document.

Sheldahl

Sheldahl's Vision

The people of Sheldahl lead by using their combined resources to meet the needs of worldwide customers who purchase flexible composite materials and interconnect components. We contribute significantly to our customer's effectiveness, efficiency and profitability by providing the best total value as measured by our customers and compared with our global competition. Total value includes, but is not limited by, our technology, ability to innovate, quality, delivery and price.

Employees enjoy an environment of trust, cooperation and opportunity where teamwork directed to satisfy customer needs is highly valued and rewarded. We strive for excellence in everything we do with dedication to constant improvement.

Our competitors consider us a role model. Our suppliers and customers value us as a long-term business partner. The local communities in which we work think of us as responsible citizens, and the financial community seeks us as a profitable investment.

Our financial performance leads our competitors and compares favorably with industry peers. When we invest in businesses, we favor those that consistently achieve a net return on total assets greater than our competition. As markets in which we participate grow, we achieve our desired market position.

Commentary

Sheldahl's leadership position is highlighted in its vision statement. Although many business-oriented principles are emphasized in the introductory and concluding paragraphs, the ethical overtones in this statement are strong. The paragraph on employees uses a number of ethics terms—trust, cooperation and teamwork. This statement is unique in articulating that the firm views itself as a role model for competitors. Other stakeholders are also specifically identified. In a letter to the author, the current CEO, James Donaghy, said: "Sheldahl's Vision was developed nine years ago by a team of leaders who wanted to transform how people think about Sheldahl. It has and continues to serve us well as a goal for our behavior."

Southern California Edison Company

Our Values

Challenge:

We will challenge ourselves to continuously improve our performance and constantly renew our understanding of our changing business.

Candor:

We will conduct ourselves with honesty, openness and integrity in all our relationships.

Commitment:

We will achieve:

◻ Value for our customers

◻ Leadership for our community and environment

◻ Excellence as a team

◻ Shared purpose with regulators, and

◻ Value for our shareholders.

Commentary

This short values statement of Southern California Edison conveys the three C's that guide the company. The "challenge" value stresses continuous improvement in the spirit of total quality management. "Candor" signifies the ethical values of the firm. Although candor was not used by other companies in this volume, it is an excellent term to convey the firm has a candid corporate culture. The "commitment" value outlines the company's responsibility to its stakeholders.

Starbucks

MISSION STATEMENT AND GUIDING PRINCIPLES
To establish Starbucks as the premier purveyor of the finest coffee in the world while maintaining our uncompromising principles as we grow.

The following six guiding principles will help us measure the appropriateness of our decisions:

- Provide a great work environment and treat each other with respect and dignity.
- Embrace diversity as essential to the way we do business.
- Apply the highest standards of excellence to the purchasing, roasting, and fresh delivery of our coffee.
- Develop enthusiastically satisfied customers all of the time.
- Contribute positively to our communities and our environment.
- Recognize that profitability is esssential to our future success.

Starbucks built on its Mission and Principles with a Framework for a Code of Conduct. Starbucks commits to do our part. The objective of the Framework was to influence the quality of life in coffee origin countries through the company's business practices. The values behind the Framework are addressed in its Beliefs.

STATEMENT OF BELIEFS

At Starbucks, we're guided by a set of simple beliefs. We start by treating each other with respect and dignity and extend this desire for fair treatment beyond our doors into our communities. As we travel the world in search of the highest quality coffee, it is our desire to do business with those who share similar values and abide by international standards for the treatment of others.

Seeing profound differences in quality of life, we've committed to doing our part to improve conditions in coffee-origin countries through self-help and educational programs. Making a

---

real difference, however, is a long-term challenge requiring the efforts of many. We will work with others in coffee-origin countries to achieve our aspirations and do our part to engage in effective action within the specialty coffee industry. We also believe that selecting and marketing high value coffee *in itself* can contribute to the economies of coffee-producing countries so that countries may improve their own quality of life.

Though our beliefs cannot be imposed upon others and these desired results may not be achieved in the near future, they form the basis of our intentions and are the foundation for our goals.

WE RESPECT HUMAN RIGHTS AND DIGNITY

We believe that people should work because they want or need to, but not because they are forced to do so.

We believe that people have the right to freely associate with whichever organizations or individuals they choose.

We believe that children should not be unlawfully employed as laborers.

WE ARE DEDICATED TO WORKING WITH OTHERS TO RAISE STANDARDS OF HEALTH, EDUCATION, WORKPLACE SAFETY, AND ECONOMIC WELL-BEING IN ALL COMMUNITIES WHERE WE DO BUSINESS.

We believe that wage and benefit levels should address the basic needs of workers and their families.

We believe that people should work in safe and healthy places that are free from hazardous conditions.

We believe that if children work, it should not interfere with mandated education.

We believe people should have access to safe housing, clean water, and health facilities and services.

WE BELIEVE IN THE POSITIVE VALUE OF DIVERSITY AND RESPECT THE INTEGRITY OF DIFFERENT CULTURES.

We believe that we should serve as a model of a successful company that promotes diversity throughout all levels.

We believe that regardless of our differences, each human being should be accorded the opportunity to meet his/her basic needs and that human rights and values should be upheld and promoted.

We believe that we should respect local laws and customs.

WE BELIEVE IN PRESERVING AND ENHANCING THE PHYSICAL ENVIRONMENT.

We believe in the importance of progressive environmental practices and conservation efforts.

We believe in demonstrating leadership for environmental practices in countries in which we do business.

We believe that hazardous materials such as chemicals and pesticides should be used safely and responsibly, if at all.

OUR COFFEE MISSION

At Starbucks, we are committed to being the premier purveyor of the finest coffee in the world as the leader of the specialty coffee industry.

We will continue to demonstrate leadership by setting high standards to which we will hold ourselves and will encourage the adoption of these by others in the coffee industry. We recognize that improving conditions internationally requires the efforts of many, and we will do our part in concert with others.

WE EXPECT TO DEMONSTRATE OUR LEADERSHIP IN THE COFFEE INDUSTRY IN THREE AREAS:

1) **Coffee Quality**—Encouraging coffee producing practices that produce the highest quality coffee.

2) **Quality of Work Life**—Improving quality of work life for those who produce, harvest, and process coffee.

3) **Environmental Quality**—Promoting sound environmental practices for production and processing coffee.

We will actively work with our partners, vendors, importers, and distributors of coffee, other coffee companies, and nonprofit organizations to improve the quality of life for those employed in growing, harvesting and processing coffee.

Commentary

Starbucks'mission and guiding principles, belief statement and coffee mission present the overall philosophy of the firm. The corporate mission speaks of "maintaining our uncompromising principles." The *belief statement focuses on the dignity of individuals *throughout the world. Both the understanding of diverse cultures and the improvement of working conditions for the workers are admirable goals outlined in the document. However, Starbucks realizes that they may not be able to change the beliefs of others (boldfaced section). The company works to implement its coffee mission through an annual work plan with specific objectives for international programs. Few ethics statements make explicit mention of human rights as this one does (Cottrill 1996). The firm's commitment to the environment is reaffirmed in the final belief statement and in the coffee mission and implemented in their stores with the use of recycled materials in packaging. Starbucks' CEO, Howard Schultz, outlined his views on the employees, the environment and human rights recently (Scott 1995).*

The Stride Rite Corporation

Values and Practices

The Stride Rite we will create builds on the foundation we have inherited, affirms the best of our Company's traditions and makes our policies and practices consistent with our principles.

Our goal is to sustain responsible financial success by achieving superior profitability. To accomplish this, we will build a Company where associates are proud and committed, and where all have an opportunity to contribute, learn, grow and advance based on merit. Associates will be respected, treated fairly, heard, involved and challenged. Above all, we want satisfaction from accomplishments, balanced personal and professional lives, to support the community, and to have fun in our endeavors.

We will make these goals a reality by being committed to new behaviors such as:

⇔ *Diversity:* Valuing a diverse workforce and diversity in experience and perspectives. Diversity will be valued and honesty rewarded.

⇔ *Recognition:* Recognizing individual and team contributions to our success. Recognition will be given to all who contribute—those who create and innovate as well as those who support the day-to-day business requirements.

⇔ *Ethical Management Practices:* Behaving in a manner consistent with the Company's high standards for business ethics, enforced throughout the Corporation.

⇔ *Communication:* Clarity regarding Company, divisional and individual goals. Associates will know what is expected and will receive ongoing communication that is timely, open, direct and honest.

⇔ *Empowerment:* Increasing the authority and responsibility of those closest to our products and customers. By empowering associates and building trust, we will encourage and unleash the full capabilities of our people.

⇔ *Risk Taking:* Encouraging and properly recognizing calculated risk-taking, regardless of the results. Openness to change will stimulate and support creative ideas and solutions.

⇔ *Customer Service:* Striving for excellence with internal and external customers.

⇔ *Career Opportunities:* Providing opportunities for career growth, where advancement within the Company becomes the normal practice, not the exception.

⇔ *Strategic Decision Making:* Anticipating and supporting change by making decisions based on long-term strategies.

⇔ *Continual Improvement:* Constantly striving for excellence and high standards by challenging old methods and offering creative solutions.

⇔ *Having Fun:* While we work very hard to achieve our goals, we must not lose sight of a very important element in our lives—having fun!

By committing to these new behaviors and showing support and trust toward all members of The Stride Rite Team, we will achieve our overall goal of commercial success.

Commentary

This document outlines the overall philosophy of the company as well as the "new behaviors" which the firm espouses. The last two sentences of the long paragraph indicate a strong commitment to employees. The new behaviors set out several admirable principles the firm plans to follow. The one on ethical management practice recognizes that "enforcement" is necessary if high ethical standards are to be a reality. Stride Rite's commitment to ethical principles is not new. In 1919, the company promised "to produce an honest quality product in an honest way and deliver it as promised." The firm's reputation as a responsible employer, a marketer with a high quality emphasis and a corporate citizen with conflicting social responsibilities has been examined in the business press (Pereira 1993; Stone 1992).

TDIndustries

At TDIndustries, we try to follow these Basic Values in all of our relationships with customers, with suppliers, within our communities, and among ourselves.

1. Concern for and Belief in Individual Human Beings
   The basic character of our group is, above all, a concern for individual human beings. We believe that the individual has dignity and importance, that people are basically honest, and that each person wants to do a good job. We believe that no one has ever really found the limits of human ability. If we draw our strength from the uniqueness of each individual, together we can become greater than the sum of our members. TD Industries is best thought of as a group of individuals—not as an impersonal "company". We, as a group, own it and do its work.

2. Valuing Individual Differences
   We will be an organization in which the full range of individual differences exist and are valued among all our stakeholders.

3. Honesty

4. Building Trusting Relationships
   We believe people react positively when trust and confidence are placed in them and when the best is expected of them. We try to reflect this belief in all our relationships.

5. Fairness
   Fairness includes equal treatment and equal opportunity for everyone.

6. Responsible Behavior
   We have high expectations of each other. We expect people to act responsibly and to work for group goals. We expect them to be dependable and to work hard.

7. High Standards of Business Ethics

Leadership

In his book *The Servant as Leader*, Robert Greenleaf successfully expressed our views of how people can and should work together to grow our company. If our organization is to live up to its Basic Values and Mission, a key ingredient will be the *Leadership* provided by a very large number of us.

Simply and plainly defined, Leaders are people who have followers. They have earned recognition and respect.

Leaders are first a servant of those they lead. They are a teacher, a source of information and knowledge, and a standard setter, more than a giver of directions and a disciplinarian.

Leaders see things through the eyes of their followers. They put themselves in others' shoes and help them make their dreams come true.

Leaders do not say, "Get going." Instead, they say, "Let's go!" and lead the way. They do not walk behind with a whip; they are out in front with a banner.

Leaders assume that their followers are working with them. They consider others partners in the work and see that they share in the rewards. They glorify the team spirit.

Leaders are people builders. They help those around them to grow because the leader realizes that the more strong people an organization has, the stronger it will be.

Leaders do not hold people down, they lift them up. They reach out their hand to help their followers scale the peaks.

Leaders have faith in people. They believe in them. They have found that others rise to their high expectations.

Leaders use their heart as well as their head. After they have looked at the facts with their head, they let their heart take a look too.

Leaders keep their eyes on high goals. They are self-starters. They create plans and set them in motion. They are persons of thought and persons of action—both dreamers and doers.

Leaders are faced with many hard decisions, including balancing fairness to an individual with fairness to the group. This sometimes requires "weeding out" those in the group who, over a period of time, do not measure up to the group needs of dependability, productivity, and safety.

Leaders have a sense of humor. They are not stuffed shirts. They can laugh at themselves. They have a humble spirit.

Leaders can be led. They are not interested in having their own way, but in finding the best way. They have an open mind.

Commentary

The TDIndustries statement is unique in its emphasis on leadership. As the prefatory material to the Leadership section indicates, this trait is essential in achieving company values. The leadership points contain an inspirational tone. The seven basic values are somewhat standard, but the focus on the individual in the first one does make an excellent point often overlooked in other values statements. Leadership's critical role in business success receives thorough treatment here and draws heavily from Greenleaf (1977).

Texas Instruments

The TI Commitment

Ethical decision-making depends upon your understanding of personal and TI values and principles coupled with good personal judgment. You, the individual, play the most important role in the ethical decision-making process and, therefore, in the ethical standards of TI. "The TI Commitment" will aid you in this process by describing our mission, our basic principles and our values.

Principles

We will accomplish this with "Excellence in everything we do"

- Perform with unquestionable ethics and integrity
- Achieve customer satisfaction through total quality
- Be a world-class technology/manufacturing leader
- Provide profitable growth/fair return on assets
- Achieve continuous improvement with measurable progress
- Be a good corporate citizen

Values

TIers expect the highest levels of performance and integrity from ourselves and each other. We will create an environment where people are valued as individuals and treated with respect, dignity, and fairness. We and team members strive to create opportunities for TIers to develop and reach their full potential and to achieve our professional and personal goals.

Ethical Decision-Making

TI policies and procedures have been developed over the years and are revised as required. While a real effort has been made to cover the questions that might be raised in the area of business ethics, no set of policies and procedures can begin to cover every situation that might arise.

Regardless of the job we do at TI, ethics and integrity are always critical in our everyday decisions:

** when reporting time worked

** when using TI resources

** when interacting with customers, suppliers and
   competitors

** when confronted with a difficult deadline

** when required to sign off that an item of work has been
   properly done

** when deciding whether to raise an ethical issue

All TIers have not only the right but the personal
responsibility to resolve any doubts or uncertainties relating to
ethical questions in the course of their duties at TI.

Commentary

*The Texas Instruments Commitment heads the company ethics
code. Its preamble focuses on ethical decision making and the fact that
the first bullet point in the principles mentions "unquestionable ethics
and integrity" seems significant. The first sentence of the values
statement reiterates this point. The "Ethical Decision-Making" section is uncommon in most codes and spells out the commitment to it
in all TI activities. These short statements are reinforced by an extensive ethics training program and an innovative e-mail based communication system concerning ethical issues called "Instant Experience"
(Trevino and Nelson 1995, 241–44).*

Thomas Cook

Our strategy is to substantially increase the profitability and value of the Thomas Cook Group by doing everything that is necessary to earn and retain the trust of our customers, our business partners, our people, and our stakeholders.

We will develop customer relationships that inspire trust. Our customers are international leisure and business travelers particularly those who prize quality and value—and those business partners who deliver our products and services to their customers with a quality consistent with our brand.

Every encounter between ourselves and our customers will enhance the trust that our customers place in us. For in these encounters we will consistently deliver the values of reliability, responsibility, and knowledge.

Our continued growth will come from the repeat business of customers who, from experience after experience, know that they can trust us above all others.

But the ability to develop relationships will depend on our recognizing that we cannot be all things to all men, and that some people - those who value price above quality, for example - are not our customers.

Commentary

This statement by Thomas Cook carries a "trust" theme. It also has a strong relationship and quality focus. This UK based firm with offices in around 100 countries obviously sees trust as the key variable in solidifying its relationships with customers. One unique, and quite commendable, feature of this document is that the company admits in the last two lines that price sensitive travelers are not likely to be its customers.

Tom's of Maine

Statement of Beliefs

WE BELIEVE that both human beings and nature have inherent worth and deserve our respect.

WE BELIEVE in products that are safe, effective, and made of natural ingredients.

WE BELIEVE that our company and our products are unique and worthwhile, and that we can sustain these genuine qualities with an ongoing commitment to innovation and creativity.

WE BELIEVE that we have a responsibility to cultivate the best relationships possible with our co-workers, customers, owners, agents, suppliers and our community.

WE BELIEVE that different people bring different gifts and perspectives to the team and that a strong team is founded on a variety of gifts.

WE BELIEVE in provi ding employees with a safe and fulfilling work environment, and an opportunity to grow and learn.

WE BELIEVE that competence is an essential means of sustaining our values in a competitive marketplace.

WE BELIEVE our company can be financially successful while behaving in a socially responsible and environmentally sensitive manner.

Mission

TO SERVE our customers by providing safe, effective, innovative, natural products of high quality.

TO BUILD a relationship with our customers that extends beyond product usage to include full and honest dialogue, responsiveness to feedback, and the exchange of information about products and issues.

TO RESPECT, value and serve not only our customers, but also our co-workers, owners, agents, suppliers, and our community; to be concerned about and contribute to their

---

well-being, and to operate with integrity so as to be deserving of their trust.

TO PROVIDE meaningful work, fair compensation, and a safe healthy work environment that encourages openness, creativity, self-discipline, and growth.

TO CONTRIBUTE to and affirm a high level of commitment, skill and effectiveness in the work community.

TO RECOGNIZE, encourage, and seek a diversity of gifts and perspectives in our work life.

TO ACKNOWLEDGE the value of each person's contribution to our goals, and to foster teamwork in our tasks.

TO BE DISTINCTIVE in products and policies which honor and sustain our natural world.

TO ADDRESS COMMUNITY CONCERNS, in Maine and around the globe, by devoting a portion of our time, talents, and resources to the environment, human needs, the arts, and education.

TO WORK TOGETHER to contribute to the long-term value and sustainability of our company.

TO BE A PROFITABLE and successful company, while acting in a socially and environmentally responsible manner.

Commentary

This firm specializes in natural personal care products. The Statement of Beliefs, while not using the word "ethics," conveys a strong moral commitment to humans, nature, stakeholders (fourth point), teamwork, competence, and responsibility. While this book has excluded most mission statements, the Tom's of Maine mission is meant to be coupled with the beliefs and is much more proactive than most others of this type. It elaborates on a number of the belief statements and ends with the same emphasis on social and environmental responsibility. These are noble goals for any firm, but indispensable to a firm marketing natural products.

TRUSTe

KEY PRINCIPLES

- INFORMED CONSENT—The right of consumers to be informed about the privacy and security consequences of an online transaction BEFORE entering into one.

- PRIVACY STANDARDS VARY ACCORDING TO CONTEXT OF USE—No single privacy standard is adequate for all situations. The group decided to delineate three levels of privacy for commercial transactions, all of which fall into the realm of "best business practices," but which offer varying levels of privacy to the end user.

THE TRUSTe MARK: BASIC GUIDELINES

Any site which bears the TRUSTe mark must meet the following basic guidelines.

Disclosure of Information
1. The service must explain and summarize its general information gathering practices.
2. The service must explain in advance what personally identifiable data is being gathered, what the information is used for, and with whom the information is being shared.
3. The user can correct and update personally identifiable information.
4. The user can request to be deleted from the site's database.

Communication Monitoring
- The service may not monitor personal communications such as e-mail or instant messages.

Display of Names and Contacts
- The service will not display or make available personally identifiable name or contact information unless it is publicly available

NO EXCHANGE (ANONYMOUS) GUIDELINES
- **Anonymous Usage**

The service will not gather or record any individual site usage.

The sole exception is for billing and system administration purposes.

- **Anonymous Transactions**

The service will not gather or record any transactional data. The sole exception is for billing and system administration purposes.

- **Anonymous Chat**

The service will not monitor public communications forums (e.g., bulletin boards or chat rooms).

- **Anonymous Tracking**

The service will not retain any personal communication tracking information (e.g., E-mail headers).

1 TO 1 EXCHANGE GUIDELINES

- **Personal Marketing Data Usage Only**

The service will not disclose individual or transaction data to third parties. Individual usage and transaction data may be used for direct customer response only.

THIRD PARTY EXCHANGE GUIDELINES

- **Outbound Marketing Data Usage**

The service may disclose individual or transaction data to third parties, provided it explains what personally identifiable information is being gathered, what the information is used for, and with whom the information is being shared.

Commentary

Truste is an organization committed to establishing trust and confidence in electronic transactions. The guidelines reprinted here address online privacy. The organization hopes to license "trustmarks" to protect the privacy of online merchants and consumers. The ethical concepts of anonymity and disclosure are spelled out above. The organization also makes the distinction between one-to-one and third-party exchanges with differing guidelines. While this material is untested, it does represent an initial step at providing an ethical electronic marketplace.

TRW, Inc.

Values

Customers

Customer satisfaction is essential. We will deliver superior value to our customers through quality, reliability and technology. We grow and prosper by serving the needs of our customers better than our competitors, while effectively controlling costs.

People

The men and women of TRW make our success possible. We encourage the involvement and reward the contribution of each employee. We value open and honest communications. We create a workplace where every employee can share a sense of ownership for TRW's success. We provide equal opportunity in our employment and promotion practices.

Quality

Quality is important in everything we do. Quality is everyone's responsibility and is achieved through continuous improvement. We routinely seek ways to do things better.

Integrity

We pursue our business interests worldwide in a socially responsible manner. We conduct our businesses in accordance with the highest standards of legal and ethical conduct. We encourage every TRW employee to participate in and support community activities.

Commentary

This four-point values statement of TRW signifies what is most important to the company. The focus is clearly on customers who are satisfied by high quality products. TRW "People" are its employees, and their importance is stressed by several key words: success, contribution, communication and equal opportunity. Quality is obviously highly valued at TRW. Finally, integrity is used to denote social responsibility, ethical conduct and community involvement. Although this values list is shorter than most in this volume, it conveys a strong sense of priority for TRW.

United Technologies Corporation

Corporate Principles

United Technologies is committed to the highest standards of ethics and business conduct. This encompasses our relationship with our customers, our suppliers, our shareowners, our competitors, the communities in which we operate, and with each other as employees at every organizational level. These commitments and the responsibilities they entail are summarized here:

Our Customers

Our primary responsibility is to those who use our products and services. We are committed to providing high quality and value, fair prices and honest transactions. We will deal both lawfully and ethically with all our customers.

Our Employees

We are committed to treating one another fairly and to maintaining employment practices based on equal opportunity for all employees. We will respect each other's privacy and treat each other with dignity and respect irrespective of age, race, color, sex, religion, or nationality. We are committed to providing safe and healthy working conditions and an atmosphere of open communication for all our employees.

Our Suppliers

We are committed to dealing fairly with our suppliers. We will emphasize fair competition, without discrimination or deception, in a manner consistent with long-lasting business relationships.

Our Shareowners

We are committed to providing a superior return to our shareowners and to protecting and improving the value of their investment through the prudent utilization of corporate resources and by observing the highest standards of legal and ethical conduct in all our business dealings.

Our Competitors

We are committed to competing vigorously and fairly for business and to basing our efforts solely on the merits of our competitive offerings.

Our Communities

We are committed to being a responsible corporate citizen of the worldwide communities in which we reside. We will abide by all national and local laws, and we will strive to improve the well-being of our communities through the encouragement of employee participation in civic affairs and through corporate philanthropy.

Gathering Competitive Information

The UTC Code of Ethics recognizes that gathering and using information related to competitors is an accepted and routine business practice. The Code provides, however, that information will be sought only when there is a reasonable belief that both receipt and use of the information is lawful.

"Competitive information" includes anything related to the competitive environment or to a competitor—for example, information related to products, markets, pricing, or business plans. This information could be drawn from published sources or could otherwise be widely available to the public. Some of this information will be oriented to a specific competitor ("competitor information"), and some competitor information would be considered "proprietary," "business confidential," or "trade secret," (this circular will use the label "proprietary") which a business would attempt to hold closely. There is no single, definitive standard used by businesses for determining what is proprietary; definitions vary by industry and indeed from enterprise to enterprise; some businesses are indiscriminate and go so far as to claim that all business information is proprietary.

UTC will respect the reasonable expectations of a business for protecting its proprietary information. Because there is no single, definitive standard for determining what is proprietary and because a business must take reasonable steps to protect its proprietary information, UTC will evaluate the receipt of information within the context of the process of information gathering rather than with reference to some fixed definition of "proprietary." In other words, how the information is gathered will indicate, ordinarily, whether it is proper to receive and use. From one extreme, information gathered from published sources clearly is permitted. At the other extreme, a "Watergate" style break-in is never permitted. While in the process of gathering information, follow two principles—

1. Do not induce a person to betray a trust by offering or giving a gift or by offering or alluding to some prospective employment or business opportunity.

2. Do not intrude on reasonable expectations of privacy or confidentiality.

In seeking examples beyond the flat prohibitions against bribes and theft, it is not possible to prepare any definitive catalog or listing of improper techniques. The nature and practices of a particular market will shape some of the standards. For example, a competitor will understand that his price will be revealed by a prospective customer who uses auction techniques in conducting competitions. Aside from the practices of any given market, businesses are expected to take steps to protect information which is considered valuable. A business which does not take steps to protect its information cannot reasonably expect others to treat it as proprietary. A competitor should not have a reasonable expectation of privacy when conversing in a public place. A business can expect, on the other hand, that its computer system will not be manipulated or monitored by a "hacker."

It is imperative to use good judgment and common sense. In analyzing a possible course of conduct, ask yourself, "Why is this information available to me?"

1. Have I done anything which coerced somebody to share information? Have I, for example, threatened a supplier by

indicating that future business opportunities will be influenced by receipt of information with respect to a competitor? Have I encouraged an employee to divulge information belonging to a prior employer when such a disclosure would conflict with an employment agreement?

2. Am I in a place where I shouldn't be? If, for example, I am a field representative with privileges to move within a customer's facility, have I gone outside the areas permitted? Have I mislead anybody in order to gain access?

3. Is the contemplated technique for gathering information invasive, such as sifting through trash or setting up an electronic "snooping" device directed at a competitor's facility from across the street?

4. Have I misled somebody in a way that the person believed sharing information with me was required or would be protected by a confidentiality agreement? Have I, for example, called and misrepresented myself as a government official who was seeking information for some official purpose? Have I misrepresented myself as a supplier (covered by a proprietary rights agreement or other confidentiality agreement) and created an impression that the information would be protected?

5. Have I done something to evade or circumvent a system intended to secure or protect information?
These illustrations, expressed in the form of questions, involve intrusive acts; such conduct must not occur.

UTC's standard of a "reasonable belief" that receipt and use is lawful does not turn solely on the personal belief of the recipient. Again, ask yourself, "Would an objective third party conclude that it was reasonable for me to believe receipt and use of information was lawful?" Whether the information has any utility or value to UTC (indeed, whether or not the information is used) is immaterial in determining whether receipt was proper.

Commentary

The United Technologies (UT) Corporate Principles delineate specific commitments to six stakeholder groups. The theme of the principles is "commitment" and the word "fair" or "fairly" is used extensively to signal how the stakeholders are to be treated. The

---

competitive information section is one of nine separate booklets on ethical issues UT has developed to provide guidance for its employees. The numbered points list many questions that should be asked. Few firms have gone to this length to instruct their personnel in dealing with the sensitive area of competitive information.

Unocal

STATEMENT OF PRINCIPLES
Unocal's Code of Conduct for doing business internationally

Meet the highest ethical standards in all of our business activities.
- Conduct business in a way that engenders pride in our employees and respect from the world community.

Treat everyone fairly and with respect.
- Offer equal employment opportunity for all host country nationals, regardless of race, ethnic group, or sex.
- Make sure that a very high percentage of the work force is made up of nationals.
- Train and develop national employees so they have full access to opportunities for professional advancement and positions at higher levels in the organization.

Maintain a safe and healthful workplace.
- As employees, value and protect each other's health and safety as highly as we do our own.

Use local goods and services as much as practical, whenever they're competitive and fit our needs.

Improve the quality of life in the communities where we do business.
- Contribute—and not just economically—to local communities, so that our presence enhances people's lives in long-lasting, meaningful ways.

Protect the environment.
- Take our environmental responsibilities seriously and abide by all environmental laws of our host country, as we do in the United States.

Communicate openly and honestly.
- Maintain our policy of encouraging meaningful dialogue with concerned shareholders, employees, the media, and members of the public.

Be a good corporate citizen and a good friend of the people of our host country.

Commentary

Unocal purposely positions this statement as being international in scope with multiple references to host countries and "nationals." The use of active tense verbs signals that the company plans to be proactive in following these principles. It appears noteworthy that several points address ethical standards—fairness, openness and honesty. This statement is unique in stating that Unocal will "contribute" to local communities. Recognition that multinationals should make lasting and meaningful contributions wherever they operate is not only an admirable goal but also, if accomplished, will minimize criticism of the firm by outsiders.

UNUM

Values

We take pride in ourselves and the organization's leadership position:

- Acting with integrity and high ethical standards
- Achieving leadership in performance, the community and the industry
- Setting and meeting individual goals consistent with business goals, and owning our individual performance
- Being motivated and excited about the organization
- Believing in what we are doing
- Emphasizing the positives, celebrating our successes and strengths, and constantly striving to improve our performance
- Delivering results

We value and respect people:

- Dealing with each other as individuals, and treating each other as we would like to be treated
- Developing people to their fullest potential
- Working together in a common endeavor: recognizing each other as an important element to the success of the whole
- Having a common understanding of each other's role and how we fit with the corporate objectives
- Collaborating with each other and having a sense of team
- Recognizing and accepting differences among people but sharing the same values

We value customers:

- Building long-term relationships with our customers and intermediaries
- Maintaining a strong orientation to service and the customer

- Delivering what we promise

We value communication:
- Communicating clearly, consistently and openly with everyone we deal with
- Building an environment which encourages open communication, participation, honesty and candor
- Listening

Commentary

Unum's four point values statement focuses on leadership, people, customers and communication. The first two values emphasize internal characteristics, while the customers one is external and the communication one has both internal and external aspects. The bullet points accentuate that the company is actively pursuing these values. The document also has an upbeat tone and opens and closes with a strong sense of ethical values.

USAA's Core Values

Service

We will give outstanding, responsive service to our members, customers and fellow employees. Our products and service will be of the highest quality and value at fair prices. We will treat others as we wish to be treated, with courtesy, dignity and respect. We will provide service to the communities in which we do business- through corporate and individual employee involvement in volunteer service and participation in the political process.

Loyalty

We will be loyal and respectful toward members and customers and toward each other, putting the Association first in the face of conflicting business interests as long as that is consistent with other ethical principles. To this end, we will safeguard confidential and proprietary information.

Honesty

We will be truthful, sincere, law-abiding, and straightforward in our communications and dealings with members and customers and with each other.

Integrity

We will consistently behave in ways that are ethical, earning the respect of members and customers by being steadfast in our commitment to act in both their best interests and the interests of the Association, regardless of any business, social, economic or personal pressures to the contrary.

© 1996

USAA is committed to the highest standards of ethics and professional conduct in day-to-day business operations as well as in interactions with our members and customers, our fellow employees, our business partners and our community. USAA corporate business activity and individual employee conduct at all levels will be consistent with our core values.

USAA's Quality Principles

- Everyone is responsible for quality because everyone has a customer.
- We take personal responsibility to meet or exceed our external and internal customers' needs and expectations.
- We must design, not inspect, quality into every process.
- We commit to continuous improvement in everything we do.
- We recognize individuals and groups for improving quality.

© 1991

The PRIDE Vision
To provide member-driven service delivery that is flexible and ever improving.

© 1992

Principles of PRIDE
(Professionalism Results In Dedication to Excellence)

Exceed member expectations—every contact is an opportunity to demonstrate our commitment to service.

Live the Golden Rule—treat others with courtesy and respect.

Be a leader—everyone can be a leader, even if you only lead yourself.

Participate and contribute—the success of USAA is everyone's responsibility.

Pursue excellence—relentlessly search for improvement.

Work as a team—teamwork promotes innovation and encourages creativity.

Share knowledge—it only reaches its full potential when shared.

Keep it simple—make it easy for our members to do business with us and for us to work together.

Listen and communicate—our customers and our coworkers want and deserve our best.

Have fun—if you're not, figure out what's stopping you, and change it.

Ethics "Quick Test"

If you have concerns or questions about a course of action, ask yourself these six questions to begin your evaluation process:

■ Is the action legal?
■ Would doing it make me feel bad?
■ Is it consistent with USAA's values and policies?
■ Would I want my parents or children to read about it in the newspaper?
■ Would failing to act make the situation worse or allow a "wrong" to continue?
■ Does it follow the "Golden Rule"?

If you still have questions or concerns, do not act until they've been raised and resolved. USAA's policy and procedures manuals, your supervisor, Human Resources, USAA's General Counsel agency or Ethics Office staff are available to help.

© 1996

Reproductions of these statements is authorized with USAA permission.

Commentary

USAA has an interesting set of ethics and quality statements. The Core Values are few, but convey both the customer and ethical focus of the firm. Their Quality Principles propose a broad interpretation of customers and an emphasis on shared responsibility to accomplish quality improvements. The Principles of PRIDE were developed after determining USAA member expectations and benchmarking with other firms. The resulting principles represent an excellent motivating guide for employees. Finally, the Ethics 'Quick Test' provides six questions for employees to deal effectively with ethical problems they may face. It is noteworthy that the Golden Rule appears both in PRIDE principles and as the last question in the quick test. The core values and quick test are the beginning and ending points of USAA's Code of Business Ethics & Conduct which spells out the firm's ethical boundaries.

VF Corporation

Code of Business Conduct

<u>Statement of Mission and Purpose</u>

VF is a diversified apparel company whose mission it is to provide above average shareholder returns by being the industry leader in marketing and servicing basic fashion apparel needs while maintaining conservative financial strategies.

The purpose of the Company is to manufacture and market products which offer superior real value to the customer and consumer compared to competition. In doing so, it is a cornerstone of our business philosophy to achieve a leadership position in every facet of our business and to judge our actions by the highest standards of excellence. We will restrict growth only by the stability and quality of profits and our ability to develop and market products offering superior value.

The Company intends to achieve profit levels sufficient to provide an attractive return to its shareholders and to provide adequate resources necessary to achieve corporate objectives.

The Company desires to provide stable employment in positions which will allow employees to develop personally and professionally. It is the Company's aim that our employees will derive satisfaction form achieving corporate objectives through superior performance in an organization environment characterized by competence, integrity, teamwork and fairness.

The conduct of business with employees, customers, consumers, suppliers, and all others shall be based on an honest, fair and equitable basis. It has been and will continue to be the Company's policy to obey the laws of each country and to honor our obligations to society by being an economic, intellectual, and social asset to each community and nation in which the Company operates.

Commentary

The VF document is an "all purpose" one. It deals with the mission, purpose and ethical beliefs of the company. Although the

---

statement begins with a strong financial emphasis, the last two paragraphs focus on the ethical ideals and stakeholders' legal responsibilities. Both the use of the paragraph format, and the multiple thrust (economic and ethical) make it a good candidate for inclusion.

Whirlpool Corporation

Shared Values

We, the people of Whirlpool aren't "in" the company, we "are" the company. As such, we recognize our individual responsibility to assure our collective success by practicing and promoting the following values. These values reflect a shared view of how we seek to operate and to be seen by others. Further, they serve as a standard for creating a climate in which we can embrace continual change and challenge worldwide.

Business with Integrity

We will pursue our business with honor, fairness and respect for both the individual and the public at large . . . ever mindful that there is no right way to do a wrong thing.

Quality as a Quest

Success depends on our ability to deliver a level of excellence respected by all who rely on us. We will lift the quality and value of our products and services above the expectations of those who receive them . . . always recognizing that our best today can be bettered tomorrow.

Customer as the Focus

We will dedicate ourselves to anticipate the changing needs of customers and to create innovative and superior products and services, faster and more effectively than can our competitors.

Commitment to the Common Good

We will serve responsibly as members of all communities in which we live and work, respecting cultural distinctions throughout the world. We will preserve the environment, prudently utilize natural resources and maintain all property we are privileged to use.

Power of Trust

A mutual and inspiring trust, nurtured by honest and open communication and equal opportunity, should unite our actions and relationships with one another . . . providing a foundation for teamwork, confidence and loyalty.

Learning to Lead

Our competitive edge in the marketplace ultimately depends on how our skills and expertise measure against the world's best. To lead the best, we must cultivate our talents through continuous training . . . confident that we will be provided every opportunity to widen our horizons.

Spirit of Winning

At the heart of company values lies company spirit. It encompasses the determination, resourcefulness, boldness and vigor by which we work. Collectively, we believe this urgent and relentless drive will enable us to shape the future of our industry . . . and deliver the performance that earns us success in the marketplace.

The Values represent a shared set of beliefs about what's important and the way we should operate to achieve the Vision. The Values also constitute a written benchmark, a clear code of conduct, by which we can measure and judge our actions. Whether they're just words on paper or truly shapers of the way our company acts, however, depends on the extent to which Whirlpool people live them each and every day.

Commentary

The Whirlpool Values Statement combines well accepted business and ethical principles. The ethical tone is set with the preamble and first statement on integrity. This one also mentions the "common good" in relating the company's responsibility to the community stakeholder. Trust is broadly defined to include open communication and equal opportunity is also noted as a central value of the firm. The final section makes an excellent comment by noting that these values represent a benchmark by which Whirlpool's actions should be judged and the company must live up to them.

Chapter 3
Beyond Ethics Statements

Developing, publicizing and reinforcing ethics statements are just the beginning. They need to be part of an integrated ethics program. Implementing ethics into an organization means making a commitment to ethical business practice. Several additional considerations warrant discussion in going beyond the ethics statement. The purpose of this chapter is to place such statements in a broader context within the overall ethical posture of an organization.

This concluding chapter covers four areas. The first presents an overall evaluation of the *Eighty Exemplary Ethics Statements*. The second section discusses several ethics programs that have evolved from the company statements. Third, challenges facing organizations as they move to the 21st century are presented. Finally, several concluding thoughts are offered.

Overall Evaluation

A number of themes emerge from examining the statements. Stakeholders are explicitly discussed in many of them. For example, the Caux Round Table, Hormel, Johnson & Johnson and others orient their statements around the stakeholder theme. In researching and contacting these companies, the author was struck by how many have multiple ethics statements in place. The most extensive are those of Levi Strauss and Company, Starbucks and USAA. Another impression coming from these statements is their variability. The implication seems to be that many avenues are available for an organization to follow in conveying ethical principles to their constituencies.

Values Statements

The most prevalent type of ethics document is the values statement (see Index A). Thirty-nine (with some companies having more than one statement) are reprinted in this book. The number of values singled out by the organizations range from a low three (Hanna Andersson) or four (AES) to as many as ten (Donnelly). Companies usually elaborate briefly on their core values with at least a phrase or a sentence.

The most frequently mentioned values are listed in Index B (while Index C categorizes the companies according to their industry). Integrity is the value noted by the most companies. It is followed by respect, quality, commitment, responsibility, trust and teamwork. In fact, Boeing calls one of their ethical policies an "Integrity Statement." Two organizations, Golden Rule Insurance and TRUSTe, have names that reflect their dominant philosophy and values. The statements of Quad/Graphics and Thomas Cook are exclusively devoted to trust.

Other values mentioned by a few companies are honesty (which appears to be supplanted by integrity), fun (denoting that work should have its lighter moments), fairness (surprisingly small number of mentions), Golden Rule (representing a timeless but significant value) and openness (a noble goal but few publicly espouse it). Fairness and openness especially seem to be subsumed under integrity in many statements.

The value of compassion was noted only by Levi Strauss. In the highly competitive and hard-nosed 1990s, more humane values such this and empathy are ones that organizations are understandably reluctant to include. Two additional values, courage (both its physical and moral dimensions are espoused) and loyalty (difficult for companies to promise in this environment), are mentioned only by the Canada Department of Defence.

Corporate Credo

The thirty-three corporate credos reprinted in this volume can be described in a number of ways (see Index A). Some are called belief statements and others use the term "principles or commitments" to describe the ethical underpinnings of the organization. As noted in Chapter 1, these tend to be longer than the values statements and contain philosophical positions of the organization. In contrast to codes of ethics, they do not codify rules or accepted standards of behavior but attempt to motivate readers by stressing the firm's responsibilities, beliefs and commitments. Like the values statements, they are not uniform in either orientation or format. The best known credos are probably Johnson & Johnson's and the Penney Idea. Some companies combine credos with values statements such as Bayer, Comerica, Hallmark, Johnson Controls, and Procter & Gamble. Several credos read like the Ten Commandments (Hanna Andersson and LEGO) while others contain much explanation of the guiding beliefs or principles (Borg-Warner and Starbucks).

Code of Ethics

The codes reprinted here range from excerpts of longer corporate codes to specific statements on various ethical issues facing organizations. About twenty fall into the code category. The ones from Caterpillar, Hershey and Marriott are part of a longer code, while Guardsmark and Levi Strauss are reprinted in their entirety. The rationale for including these is that they are among the best developed statements about corporate ethics.

Specific topical areas covered by these codes include: privacy (Canadian Direct Marketing Association and DHL Systems), sexual harassment (Hyatt), equal opportunity concerns (Nalco), gift giving and receiving (General Motors), and political advertising (Campaign Advertising). The rationale for the particular directives is that the issues are germane to these companies.

While these codes can generally be applauded, other companies have made changes to their codes of ethics during the 1990s that were not always positive. The author is aware of a major corporation which has made its code "leaner and meaner" by deleting sections such as one on not disparaging competitors to deal with the highly competitive environment the company faces. Other problems with codes is that they are too short to contain meaningful guidance for employees or too platitudinous to be realistically followed. As mentioned in Chapter 1, all codes should contain guidance as to enforcement and direction (see Nortel and Sears).

Corporate Ethics Programs

As mentioned above, promulgating, promoting and enforcing ethics statements are just a start. Many organizations have developed extensive corporate ethics training programs to instill higher standards of behavior in their employees. Some impetus came from the Federal Sentencing Guidelines that were introduced in the early 1990s. However, many organizations see both short- and long-term payoffs in having a strong ethics program. Integrity-based programs are generally believed to be superior to compliance-based ones (Paine 1994).

Ethical transgressions of major companies are widely chronicled in the media. Should a company run into problems, a several step process has been suggested by France (1996), and is shown in Exhibit 1. Many large U.S.-based corporations are currently at steps 3, 4 or 5, including a number whose statements are reprinted here.

Exhibit 1
How to Conduct an Ethics Overhaul
Here's the step-by-step approach the pros usually advise:

STEP ONE: Hire an "independent" investigator to issue a report on the misconduct. Credible former government officials are preferred.

STEP TWO: Write a new ethics policy. Deliver the document to all company employees with memo from CEO instructing them not to ignore it.

STEP THREE: Expand training. Hire consultants, buy more videotapes, start scheduling regular informational sessions on subjects such as sexual harassment, bribery, etc.

STEP FOUR: Install a whistle-blowers' hotline. Publicize the phone number to employers and establish and detail fully a systematic complaint procedure.

STEP FIVE: Hire a full-time ethics officer. It's this person's job to investigate whistle-blower complaints, supervise training programs, and update the ethics policy.

Source: France (1996), 26–27.

Several ethics programs in place at some of these firms are well known and chronicled elsewhere. They are: Johnson & Johnson (Williams and Murphy 1990), Levi Strauss & Company (Mitchell 1994), Starbucks (Scott 1995) and Texas Instruments (Ferrell and

Fraedrich 1997; Trevino and Nelson 1995) Other companies have less known, but rather extensive, programs. The ones featured here are those of Bayer, Guardsmark, Sears and United Technologies.

Bayer Corporation, the U.S. subsidiary of German-based Bayer AG, instituted the Vision, Values and Beliefs (VVB) statement in 1992 (shown in Chapter 2) and viewed its development as the initial step in a full-fledged ethics program. The company embarked on a major ethics training initiative in 1995 called the Corporate Compliance Program. Several cases taken from actual situations were written and then presented to senior management using CD-ROM technology. After input by top executives, the cases were revised to be more applicable to Bayer employees. Starting in 1996 the company trained over thirty employees to lead ethics programs at their corporate sites in the United States. An important element of the training was the instruction on applying the VVB statement to the cases. Over 2,500 Bayer middle and upper management participated in day long ethics training sessions. The program was well received by virtually all participants

With the success of its VVB, training sessions and overall consciousness raising regarding ethics, the company decided to institute a new office called the corporate ombudsman in mid-1997. The responsibilites of this position are threefold: (1) to serve as a department neutral representative who tries to resolve ethical concerns of employees, (2) to handle hot line calls and provide appropriate follow up and (3) to direct further ethics training throughout the company.

Guardsmark was founded in 1963 and now employs over 12,000 people in the security services business. One of the hallmarks of the company was its decision in the 1970s to disarm its security officers. The company's code of ethics was instituted in 1980 and is believed to be the first in its industry to adopt such a statement. The extensive code is reprinted in Chapter 2. The company was a recipient of the 1996 American Business Ethics Awards from the American Society of Chartered Life Underwriters and Chartered Financial Consultants (other recipients of this award whose statements appear in the book are Hanna Andersson, Levi Strauss, Rich Products, Starbucks and Texas Instruments). Guardsmark was honored for its "uncompromising dedication to excellence and unflinching commitment to the highest ethical standards."

The company received this award for several reasons. First, starting in 1992 a "sunset clause" was added to the code, meaning that it must be thoroughly evaluated every year. The officers then sign the code. These signatures are reprinted on the back of the document. Second, the company extensively promotes its code—in employment applications, in several policy and training manuals and displayed conspicuously in the over 100 company offices. Third, the Code itself is very detailed and provides substantial guidance for employees confronted with ethical dilemmas. Fourth, the company has demonstrated the importance of ethics by placing an executive, Stephen Kasloff, in charge of ethics. He noted that the code and program both help to build trust in the company and assist in carrying out the organizational mission. Finally, and significantly, Ira Lipman, the CEO, has displayed substantial leadership within the firm and in the industry. In his acceptance of the ABEA Award he said:

> Our company is not perfect. No company is. But we try constantly to raise the bar—not only on performance, but also on expectations. That dynamic process is working, because each year we find that our Code of Ethics and our ethics program—which were as perfect as we could make them the previous year—are no longer satisfactory. By constantly raising the bar, we strive to establish ever higher standards both for our own company and for the entire private security industry.

Sears, the well known retailer, has an extensive ethics program. Its statement on professional selling in Chapter 2 is just one facet of the "values driven ethics initiative" in place at the company. Ethics is incorporated into new employee orientation programs with dissemination of its ethics booklets and through a short video. The entire initiative is under the direction of the Office of Ethics and Business Policy headed by a Vice President.

The company began a new ethics program in 1997 around the theme of "transformation," which was to be achieved through communication, personalization and implementation. The booklet outlining the company position includes the shared beliefs and the company code of business conduct outlining company policies, and features questions and answers and leadership principles delineating Sears' managers guides to practices across a range of topics such as buying and merchandising, the environment, human resources and marketing/advertising.

Top management at Sears has also taken the lead in focusing on ethics. Arthur Martinez, the CEO, has spoken often of the central role that ethics must play at Sears. In a recent speech, Mr. Martinez advocated five rules.

- Keep it simple . . . do right things for right reasons.
- Don't write rules for every contingency . . . provide broad guidelines.
- Call balls and strikes . . . be decisive regarding ethical behavior.
- Trust your people to do the right thing.
- Partner with your stakeholders for internal and external alliances.

He has encouraged his managers to instill ethics in their respective units. One approach that is used is to create values statements for major departments. Jane Thompson, President of Sears Home Services is "a strong believer in values statements" and the Credit Group's, which she formerly headed, statement embraces integrity, fairness, openness and mutual respect" (Chandler 1997).

United Technologies Corporation is a diversified company with major subsidiaries including Pratt & Whitney, Carrier, Otis and UT Automotive. The firm has had an ethics program in place for a number of years. What is unique about their program is that they not only have an overall code of ethics but also provide detailed guidance to all employees of the firm, with booklets outlining the company policies in fourteen areas such as the global economy, conflicts of interest, gift giving and the one reprinted in this volume on competitive intelligence gathering. The code has been reprinted in 22 languages. The number of different ethics statements and the fact that there are over 120 individuals worldwide designated to deal with ethical issues are distinctive.

A second important fact is that the UTC ethics initiative is overseen by two offices and executives. The Vice President of Business Practices has formal responsibility for ethics training and complying with legal as well as ethical requirements. The Corporate Ombudsman solicits anonymous comments from employees through a program called "Dialog." In the past two years the Business Practice office has received over 2,400 inquiries while the Ombudsman has had over 44,000 questions submitted to it. The extensiveness of these inputs indicates that these offices have been successful in reaching out to employees who have ethical questions.

Future Ethical Challenges

Although the statements reprinted in this book deal with a wide array of ethical issues facing organizations, several challenges are facing companies as we move toward the 21st century. The most significant international issue is human rights. Two statements reprinted here, Levi Strauss and Company and Starbucks, deal with this topic. However, many global companies are deciding what to do about their workers in third world countries. The same criticisms leveled against companies 25 years ago about their codes being too general and not enforceable are being targeted at even the exemplary firms in the 1990s by the activist critics (Cottrill 1996). The working conditions of especially young employees and the monitoring of them are ongoing sources of concern. The critics want independent monitoring rather than the audits being conducted by Levi Strauss and other firms at present. The publication of ethics statements regarding human rights is a first step, and the companies that have done so are to be applauded. But the pressure will increase on many firms to add this area to their international codes in the future.

On the domestic front several issues such as privacy, diversity and work and family issues are receiving greater discussion in the media. The increased ability in organizations to communicate electronically with one another via e-mail, voice mail and storing data and files in computers raise a host of ethical issues. Most companies have yet to address privacy and technology concerns in codes or other ethics statements. One exception is DHL Systems, whose code is reprinted in this book. The privacy of outside stakeholders is also an ongoing concern (see Canadian Direct Marketing Association code). Companies must begin to address the privacy concerns of both workers and external constituencies in the near future. This is likely an area that will warrant a specific ethics statement or an expansion of the code of ethics to deal with privacy concerns.

The diversity of the workforce as well as consuming public is well chronicled. Companies are under less legal pressure at the moment to deal with diversity topics, but it may warrant a statement of ethical principles. Several firms (First Bank, Herman Miller and Stride-Rite) listed it as a core value of the corporation, but they are in the minority. Dealing effectively with diversity issues will continue to challenge corporate executives in the future. Companies that have not developed specific principles regarding hiring, evaluating and promoting the diversity in their work force will be challenged to do so in the near future. Both managing and nurturing diversity (Capowski 1996 and Nelton 1995) are ongoing ethical issues.

The final challenge facing U.S.-based companies in the near future is the balance between the work life and family life. This has been a growing concern for employees over time. However, with the increasing number of mothers in the workforce at present, the issue has reach near crisis proportions in some circles. While it may not be necessary for companies to offer designated ethics statements on this topic, it is a serious workplace issue for managers and employees alike. Flex time, telecommuting and shared positions are all responses that companies have offered to workers seeking more of a balance or an opportunity to work part time rather than full time. Several companies whose statements are reprinted here have been singled out as among the "Top Ten" companies in family-friendliness. They are Hewlett-Packard, Marriott, Merrill Lynch and UNUM (Hammonds 1996).

Concluding Thoughts

While ethics statements play an important role in setting the overall tone for any organization, they do not supplant "people" who make ethical decisions on a daily basis. As a way to conclude this volume, a few comments need to be made about people at all levels of the organization and fostering ethical behavior.

Exhibit 2 depicts seven brief comments about people and their role in organizations. Although these needs are not ordered in a hierarchical sense, they are motivators for employees. All of these points are reflected in some of the ethical statements reprinted in this book. However, the exhibit points out the challenges to management in developing people. The message here is that people must be respected and challenged for them to be effective

---

Exhibit 2
The Needs of People

□ **People need *individual respect*.** Taking time to identify uniqueness in each person not only shows care, but generates pervasive appreciation for "real" people at work, people with hobbies, families and dreams.

□ **People need *challenge*.** The best challenges come as questions, not commands: "How would you. . . ?" is an inviting and challenging phrase to launch solutions to new business problems.

□ **People need *growth*.** The right training seminar or developmental assignment can often ignite new possibilities with unexpected business results.

□ **People need *enthusiasm*.** Ralph Waldo Emerson said that "nothing great ever was achieved without enthusiasm."

□ **People need *ethics*.** Every day, managers can sense what's not right about the workplace and then try to fix it. Such a standard can reverberate throughout the workplace.

□ **People need *balance*.** It's the balance of work against other interests that refreshes minds.

□ **People need a wide array of *reward*s.** Current research shows that people seek rewards in literally *thousands* of ways. The permutations are endless for finding a "compensation package" to create a sense of satisfaction for a job well done for all the different people who work in your company.

Source: Adapted from Brown (1996), 89.

---

in the workplace. Opportunities for growth will likely lead to enthusiasm. The point about ethics is affirmed throughout this volume. The importance of balance is stressed in Exhibit 2 and should consistently be on the minds of managers who expect their employees to perform at a high level daily. People are not unidimensional and need to seek balance in their lives. Finally, rewards must be broadly defined. It is often stated that "ethics is its own reward," but just as financial and psychic rewards are important, ethical ones should be factored in as well.

While meeting the "needs" of people is a responsibility of all managers or administrators in an organization, high executives have ultimate responsibility. The leadership of top managers is essential if ethical conduct is to pervade the organization. This writer and a colleague (Murphy and Enderle, 1995) provided illustrations of four outstanding leaders of companies: Cadbury Schweppes, Cummins, Herman Miller and Johnson & Johnson. These leaders made the ethics statement of their organization come alive and all understood the importance of "people" in furthering corporate goals and enhancing the culture.

A second theme that needs to be emphasized is that people within organizations must behave ethically when confronted with dilemmas. Several companies (Hershey, Texas Instruments and USAA) include a procedure for making ethical decisions within their organization as part of the ethics statement. While the statements reprinted in this book generally outline principles and philosophies of the organization, only those that are categorized as codes provide concrete guidance. None of these statements by themselves can assure that individuals within the organization will in fact make the correct decision from an ethical point of view.

Making ethical decisions is the overriding reason for putting in place any ethics statement. Decision making in the contemporary business environment is often complex and confusing. Exhibit 3 presents a short parable that indicates individuals will often be given conflicting advice. The outcome should ideally be a decision that is "informed, consistent and fair" and the advice is to consult with advisors and the code of ethics. (The only minor criticism this writer would have is that simplifying the code may not be as essential as having a code that is relevant for the organization—see the 80 above in Chapter 2.) The final line does give an excellent directive that individuals ultimately have to make on their own and have the moral courage to stand by it.

As a final conclusion, I offer several recommendations based on earlier research (Murphy 1988; 1989) and in assembling the ethics statement for this book. They are as follows:

- **There is no single ideal approach to corporate ethics.** The variety of statements reprinted here shows that many avenues may lead to the destination of effective ethics

---

Exhibit 3
Decision Making and Ethics

One day a father and son were walking down the road leading their horse. They came to a village, and the people there called them fools for leading the horse instead of riding it. So, the father rode the horse and the son lead, but at the next village the people called the father heartless for making the son walk. Therefore, the father put his son on the horse and began to lead it, but the people of the third village called the son cruel for making his poor father walk. Confused, they decided to both ride the horse; at the fourth village, the people said they were mean to make the horse carry both of them. Frustrated, both of them got off the horse, threw it in the river and continued on their way. At the fifth village, the folks said, "How foolish—they had a horse and threw it away." The father and son shrugged their shoulders and decided that they would stop trying to "please all the people all of the time."

This folk story illustrated how whimsical humanity can be, using something as simple as the ethical utility of a horse. Thus, it follows that people will have many opinions regarding ethics and morality. The challenge is to not be swayed by the various opinions and influences of others. You need to simplify your code of ethics, consult with a few trusted advisors and try to make an informed, consistent and fair decision.

Don't throw your horse in the river, make your own decision and have the strength to stick with it.

Source: Peterson (1997).

---

statements and programs. I would recommend that a small firm start with a credo or values statement, but a larger organization should develop a tailored code and some type of ethical program to support it (for advice in developing one, see Murphy 1989, Nash 1995, Osborne 1990).

- **Ethics statements must be more than legal or public relationship documents.** They must provide specific, meaningful and useful guidance to employees. Firms are urged to rethink their current code and incorporate some of the issues such as diversity, human rights and privacy into any further revisions.

- **Visible signs must exist that ethics matters to the organization.** This task can be accomplished by spending time in formal meetings discussing the ethics statement, issues arising from them and how the corporate culture influences ethical decisions within the unit or overall organization.

- **Top management must be committed and pay attention to detail.** Senior managers must champion the highest ethical standards for their companies. CEO letters, speeches and other public proclamations should reinforce ethical values. Top managers should also scrutinize how results are accomplished. A microscope is often used to study costs, while rising profits may not receive the same attention. If the results appear to be "too good to be true," they may be.

- **Developing a statement is not sufficient by itself.** The ethics statement, even if an exemplary one, is not useful unless supported by institutionalized managerial processes. Some of these are outlined in the four examples provided earlier in this chapter.

- **Raising the ethical consciousness of an organization is not easy.** Virtually every company whose statement is reprinted here has spent countless hours—and substantial amounts of money—developing, discussing, revising and communicating its ethical principles to employees. However, there are no guarantees that it will work. No doubt, several companies mentioned in this volume will be criticized for ethical transgressions in the near future. However, this potential downside certainly does not outweigh the value that can be gained from attempts to improve the firm's ethical posture.

- **Ethics needs a champion.** Someone must make ethics an issue of paramount concern in the organization. It is essential that the CEO be in support of ethics statements and programs, but in many organizations individuals at lower levels have championed the cause. Ethics will only improve if individuals take responsibility for it. The ethics champion in your organization could be you!

Bibliography

Alburty, Stevan. (1997). "The Ad Agency to End All Ad Agencies." *Fast Company* (December-January), 116–24.

Brown, Tom. (1996). "Sweatshops of the 1990s." *Management Review* (August), 13–18.

Cadbury, Sir Adrian. (1987). "Ethical Managers Make Their Own Rules." *Harvard Business Review* (September-October), 69–73.

Capowski, Genevieve. (1996). "Managing Diversity." *Management Review*, (June), 13–19.

Chandler, Susan (1997). "If Its On the Fritz, Take it to Jane," *Business Week*, (January 27), 74–76.

Cottril, Ken. (1996). "Global Codes of Conduct." *Journal of Business Strategy* (May/June), 55–59.

De Pree, Max. (1989). *Leadership is an Art.* (New York: Dell Trade Paperback).

De Pree, Max. (1992). *Leadership Jazz.* (New York: Currency Doubleday).

Ferrell, O. C., and John Fraedrich. (1997). *Business Ethics: Ethical Decision Making and Cases.* 3rd ed. (Boston: Houghton Mifflin Company).

Fites, Donald V. (1996). "Make Your Dealers Your Partners." *Harvard Business Review* (March-April), 84–95.

Foster, Timothy R.V. (1993). *101 Great Mission Statements: How the World's Leading Companies Run their Businesses* (London, England: Kogan Page Limited).

France, Mike (1996). "Ethics For Hire," *Business Week*, (July 15), 26–28.

Bibliography

Fritzsche, David J. (1997). *Business Ethics: A Global and Managerial Perspective* (New York: The McGraw-Hill Companies, Inc.).

Greengard, Samuel. (1996). "Privacy: Entitlement or Illusion?" *Personnel Journal*, (May), 74–88.

Greenleaf, Robert K. (1977). *Servant Leadership: A Journey Into the Nature of Legitimate Power and Greatness.* (New York: Paulist Press.)

Greenwood, John. (1997). "The Guardians." *The Financial Post 500*, 40–50.

Hamilton, Joan O'C. (1996). "David Packard: Silicon Valley's Class Act." *Business Week* (April 8), 42.

Hammonds, Keith H. (1996). "Balancing Work and Family." *Business Week*, (September 16), 74–80.

Hong Kong Ethics Development Centre (1996). *Corporate Code of Conduct.*

Jones, Patricia and Larry Kahaner. (1995). *Say It & Live It: 50 Corporate Mission Statements That Hit the Mark* (New York: Doubleday).

Katz, Jane Palley, and Lynn Sharp Paine. (1994). "Levi Strauss & Co.: Global Sourcing." Harvard Business School (Boston, MA: Harvard Business School Publishing).

Kuczmarski, Susan Smith, and Thomas D. Kuczmarski. (1995). *Values-Based Leadership* (Englewood Cliffs, NJ: Prentice Hall).

Lablich, Kenneth. (1996). "How to Fire People and Still Sleep at Night." *Fortune* (June 10), 65–72.

Laczniak, Gene R., and Patrick E. Murphy. 1993. *Ethical Marketing Decisions: The Higher Road* (Upper Saddle River, NJ: Prentice Hall).

Lancaster, Hal. (1997). "You Have Your Values: How Do You Identify Your Employer's?" *The Wall Street Journal.* (April 8), B1.

Liebig, James E. (1994). *Merchants of Vision: People Bringing New Purpose and Values to Business* (San Francisco, CA: Berrett-Koehler Publishers).

Mavrinac, Sarah C., Paine, Lynn Sharp, Eccles, Robert G., and Charles A. Nichols III. (1994). "AES Honeycomb." Harvard Business School (Boston: Harvard Business School Publishing).

Mitchell, Russell. (1994). "Managing By Values: Is Levi Strauss Approach Visionary—Or Flaky?" *Business Week* (August 1), 46–52.

Murphy, Patrick E. (1995). "Corporate Ethics Statements: Current Status and Future Prospects." *Journal of Business Ethics,* (September), 14: 726–40.

Murphy, Patrick E. (1989). "Creating Ethical Corporate Structures." *Sloan Management Review* (Winter), 81–87.

Murphy, Patrick E. (1994). "European Managers' Views on Corporate Ethics." *Business Ethics: A European Review* (July), 137–44.

Murphy, Patrick E. (1988). "Implementing Business Ethics." *Journal of Business Ethics,* (December), 907–15.

Murphy, Patrick E., and Georges Enderle. (1995). "Managerial Ethical Leadership: Examples Do Matter." *Business Ethics Quarterly* (January), 117–28.

Murphy, Patrick E., Wood, G., and G.R. Laczniak. (1996). "Relationship Marketing = Ethical Marketing," in ESOMAR/EMAC Symposium, U. Schoneberg, ed., *Research Methodologies For 'The New Marketing'* (Amsterdam, The Netherlands: ESOMAR), 21–40.

Nahser, F. Byron. (1997). *Learning to Read the Signs: Reclaiming Pragmatism in American Business.* (Boston: Butterworth-Heinemann).

Nash, L.N. (1988). "Johnson & Johnson Credo," in *Corporate Ethics: A Prime Business Asset,* J. Keogh, ed. (New York: The Business Roundtable), 93–104.

Nash, L.N. (1995). "The Real Truth About Corporate 'Values'." *Public Relations Strategist,* (Summer), 7–13.

Nelton, Sharon. (1995). "Nuturing Diversity." *Nation's Business,* (June), 13–19.

Oliverio, M. E. (1989). "The Implementation of a Code of Ethics: The Early Effort of One Entrepreneur." *Journal of Business Ethics* Vol. 8, 367–74.

Osborne, Richard L. (1991). "Core Value Statements: The Corporate Compass." *Business Horizons* (Sepember-October), 28–34.

Paine, Lynn Sharp. (1994). "Managing for Organizational Integrity." *Harvard Business Review*, (March/April), 106–17.

Pepper, John E. (1997). "The Boa Principle: Operating Ethically in Today's Business Environment." Florida A&M University, January 30.

Pereira, Joseph. (1993). "Split Personality: Social Responsibility and Need for Low Cost Clash at Stride Rite." *The Wall Street Journal.* (May 28), A1.

Peterson, Casey C. (1997). "Ethics Corner." *It's Your Money* (Summer), 3.

Scott, Mary. (1995). "Howard Schultz." *Business Ethics*, (November/December), 26–29.

Singer, Andrew W. (1993). "Democracy Plus Fairness Equals Productivity at Donnelly Corporation." *Ethikos* 6 (5): 13 and 16.

Stern, Gabriella and Joann S. Lublin. (1996). "New GM Rules Curb Wining and Dining." *The Wall Street Journal* (June 5), B1.

Stone, Nan. (1992). "Building Corporate Character: An Interview with Stride Rite Chairman Arnold Hiatt." *Harvard Business Review* (March-April), 95–104.

Trevino, Linda K., and Katherine A. Nelson. (1995). *Managing Business Ethics: Straight Talk About How To Do It Right.* (New York: John Wiley).

Williams, Oliver F., and Patrick E. Murphy. (1990). "The Ethics of Virtue: A Moral Theory for Marketing," *Journal of Macromarketing* (Spring), 19–29.

Index A
Statements Index

CODE OF ETHICS

ETHICAL ISSUES IN CODES

Index B
Values Index

INTEGRITY

AES	Hanna Andersson
Baxter	Hewlett Packard
Binney & Smith	Johnson Controls
Boeing	Levi Strauss
Cadbury Schweppes	Mary Kay
Ciba	Merrill Lynch
Coachmen	Nahser
Cummins	Nortel
Ethyl	Procter & Gamble
First Bank	Progressive
General Moters	TRW
Golden Rule	UNUM
GPU	Whirlpool

LEADERSHIP

Cummins	Mary Kay
Ethyl	Procter & Gamble
First Bank	TDIndustries
Levi Strauss	Unum

OPENNESS

Cadbury Schweppes	Herman Miller
Ciba	Unocal
GPU	

QUALITY

Autodesk	Hallmark
Baxter	Hormel
Bayer	Mary Kay
Cadbury Schweppes	Protective Life
Caux Round Table	Rich Products
Coachmen	Thomas Cook
Cummins	TRW
Ethyl	Unocal
First Bank	USAA
Fisher & Paykel	Whirlpool

RESPECT

Autodesk
Baxter
Boeing
Canada Dept. of Defence
Canadian Direct Mktg
CMS Energy
Donnelly
Ethyl
GPU
Guardsmark
Hanna Andersson

Hewlett Packard
Levi Strauss
Marriott
Merrill Lynch
Nahser
Rockwell
Saturn
Starbucks
Tom's of Maine
UNOCAL

RESPONSIBILITY

AES
Bayer
Borg-Warner Security
Cadbury Schweppes
Canada Dept. of Defence
Caterpillar
Ciba

Ethyl
Guardsmark
Hanna Andersson
Herman Miller
Levi Strauss
Nahser
Nortel

TEAMWORK

Autodesk
Baxter
Donnelly
General Motors
GPU
Herman Miller
Hewlett Packard

Levi Strauss
Mary Kay
Merrill Lynch
Quad Graphics
Saturn
USAA

TRUST

Caux Round Table
A.G. Edwards
Fisher & Pykel
GPU
Guardsmark
Hewlett Packard
Hormel

Levi Strauss
Procter & Gamble
Quad/Graphics
Saturn
TDIndustries
Thomas Cook
TRUSTe

Index C
Industry Index

CHEMICALS
Bayer Corporation
Ciba Specialty Chemicals
Ethyl Corporation
Nalco
Unocal

CHILDREN'S
Binney & Smith
Hanna Andersson
LEGO
Stride-Rite

COMPUTER/TECHNOLOGY
Autodesk
DHL Systems
Hewlett Packard
TRUSTe

CONFECTIONERY
Cadbury Schweppes
Hershey Foods

CONSTRUCTION
Caterpillar
Reell Precision Manufacturing
TDIndustries

CONSUMER PRODUCTS
Hallmark
Procter & Gamble

DIVERSIFIED
TRW
United Technologies

ELECTRONICS
Sheldahl
Texas Instruments

ETHICS CENTERS
Caux Round Table
Halakhic Code
Hong Kong Centre

FINANCIAL
Centura Banks
Co-Operative Bank
Comerica
First Bank System
USAA

FOOD AND BEVERAGE
Cadbury Schweppes
Hormel Food
Kroger
Rich Products
Starbucks

HEALTH CARE
Baxter
Johnson & Johnson

HOSPITALITY
Hyatt
Marriott

INSURANCE
Golden Rule
Progressive Corporation
Protective Life
UNUM
USAA